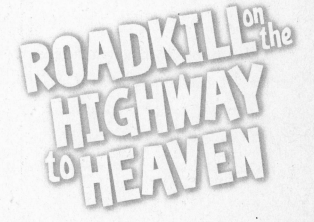

Other Books by Chonda Pierce

It's Always Darkest Before the Fun Comes Up

Chonda Pierce on Her Soapbox

I Can See Myself in His Eyeballs

Chonda Pierce

ROADKILL on the HIGHWAY to HEAVEN

no animals were injured in the writing of this book!

ZONDERVAN®

GRAND RAPIDS, MICHIGAN 49530 USA

ZONDERVAN.COM/
AUTHORTRACKER

ZONDERVAN™

Roadkill on the Highway to Heaven
Copyright © 2006 by Chonda Pierce

Requests for information should be addressed to:
Zondervan, *Grand Rapids, Michigan 49530*

Library of Congress Cataloging-in-Publication Data

Pierce, Chonda.
    Roadkill on the highway to heaven / Chonda Pierce.
       p. cm.
    ISBN-13: 978-0-310-23527-9
    ISBN-10: 0-310-23527-8
    1. Pierce, Chonda. 2. Christian biography—United States. 3. Humorists,
American—Biography. 4. Christian life—Anecdotes. I. Title.
    BR1725.P514A3 2006
    242.02'07—dc22

                                            2006004765

Published in association with the literary agency of Wolgemuth & Associates, Inc.

Unless otherwise marked, Scripture quotations are from the *Holy Bible: Today's New International Version*®. TNIV®. Copyright © 2001, 2005 by International Bible Society. Used by permission of Zondervan. All rights reserved.

Interior design by Beth Shagene

Printed in the United States of America

06 07 08 09 10 11 12 • 19 18 17 16 15 14 13 12 11 10 9 8 7 6 5 4 3 2 1

Contents

Part 6
Homeward Bound

Foreword

*W*e have a routine when it's time for my wife to go on the road. First of all, I'll drag out a suitcase from the attic, digging it out of the fiberglass insulation much like an archeologist unearths a T. rex femur bone. Then I'll go check the weather in the city she's going to and report back so she'll know how to pack.

For years now, Chonda has lugged around suitcases that were always too heavy and worn shoes that were never made for traveling. I've kissed her goodbye as she's headed out in rain, in snow, with sleep in her eyes, and with a bad case of postnasal drip. She's hit the road shortly after the announcement of bad news—like, "We've found a suspicious-looking spot." And I've watched her leave with a pocketful of antibiotics to fight off a nasty flu. If I had a nickel for every time I said, "If I knew all the punch lines, I'd go tell the jokes for you," I'd have a lot of nickels.

When Chonda leaves, I circle on the calendar the date when she's coming home, and then cross out the days as they pass, like kids do when they've got Christmas in their sights. I've met her by myself at the airport with flowers and posters (Happy Anniversary! Happy Birthday!) and at other times with our children and flowers and posters (Happy Mother's Day!). I love her when she comes home early and she's still wearing that last flashy outfit she bought because she thought it was "funky." I also love her when she has a 6 a.m. flight and has to go "hag head"—with a ball cap pulled low over her eyes—and wearing sweatpants. I think I love her the most, though, when I see her drag herself off the bus, decked in winter flannel, wearing fuzzy slippers and fuzzy hair and fuzzy teeth, and feel her way through the front door and along a path through the furniture that will take her straight to bed.

My wife is a woman with a strong sense of commitment: she watches calendars and clocks and the Weather Channel. And she's a woman with a great sense of mission: she prays for the world and then she calls home and prays with her children (usually after I say something like, "Kids? What kids?").

She's Super Traveler. She works the crossword puzzles in the back of the flight magazines, and she can draw out, from memory, the floor plan of any of the major hotel chains. When I travel with her, she's nearly impossible to keep up with in airports. I usually have to hitch a ride on one of those golf carts and then say to the driver something like, "Follow that blonde streak!"

Chonda is an incredible wife and an incredible mother. She works way too hard and takes a beating out there on the road. She may laugh a lot about being roadkill, like a possum gone belly up. Truth is, I've seen her come pretty close to being just that recently, and that scared me. Now I make her slow down, look both ways before crossing the road, and say no more often. I travel with her as much as possible. And together we are in search of the world's most comfortable pair of traveling shoes.

This Tennessee boy has seen a lot of roadkill in his time, so believe me when I say there's none out there in all this world that I would rather kiss than my wife, Chonda.

Now be careful and come home soon. I love you.

—David

P.S. Are the kids with you?

Introduction
How I Came to Love Roadkill

*M*y first experience with roadkill came at an early age. I was a little girl riding in the backseat of the car on a long family trip from Kentucky to South Carolina.

"Let's play the counting game," my older sister, Charlotta, said.

I'd played this game before. What you do is pick an object and then count that object all the way to your destination. The key to winning is to pick an object that you've got a good chance to see a lot of, like a water tower or a school bus—not something like a three-legged dog. (I think my brother, Mike, picked that one year so he wouldn't have to play along.) This particular year, I chose to count green cars. Charlotta picked towns beginning with the letter *C*. Mike chose tractors. (Remember, we were driving from Kentucky to South Carolina, through Tennessee.) My little sister, Cheralyn, said, "I'm going to count dead hogs in the road." (Remember, we were driving from Kentucky to South Carolina, through Tennessee.) I believe she counted three.

I'm all grown up now, and wouldn't you know it, I live in Tennessee —home of tractors and dead hogs! The state that passed a "roadkill law" a few years ago, which basically says if you kill it with your car, you can keep it. I can remember all the hoopla on the local news when this law was debated. Someone actually went out and made some video of Tennessee roadkill. What I learned from that video is that there is no decent way to photograph a squashed possum. I still have a nightmarish image of one of the creatures splayed out flat on its back, its body wracked and its pink tongue lolling out the side of its mouth. Then one day—just outside of Cincinnati, I think—I had an epiphany: There are days when I feel just like that squashed possum. I totally identified with the roadkill.

Telling jokes around the country, believe it or not, is hard work. I have to fly for hours, I have to take a bus for days, I have to walk up steep stairs in skinny heels. In short, I sometimes take a beating. I get squashed and sideswiped and—well, you get the picture. Yet with all the trials and tribulations on the road, every now and then I'll get run over by a victory, a moment when God comes down and shows his glory. That's what keeps me going.

The road has been tender to me and brutal to me. Perhaps it has been to you as well. I've traveled many miles, but you don't always have to travel a long ways from home to find a struggle, do you? Perhaps you're feeling a bit like roadkill yourself—from laps you take to and from work, from running family errands in the minivan, or from calorie-burning strolls through your neighborhood. The road's the road, right?

One night on the road, I began to write back to my family about what I had seen and learned—the good, the bad, and the ugly. At first I called these "my letters to home." (Boring!) Then one day, with my tongue lolling out to the side and my body travel weary, I referred to my letter as the "Roadkill Report." The name stuck.

My tour bus is forty-one feet long and twenty tons of steel, plastic, and faux wood. On a bus, you can eat, sleep, and shower at seventy miles per hour. If that isn't a recipe for roadkill, I don't know what is. On a moving bus, things break — dishes, TVs, bones. On a bus, things smell. (I won't list what I think those might be.) On a bus, you fall asleep at night in one town and wake up hundreds of miles away in another town. Who knows what you may have run over along the way? More than once I've lain in my bunk, toes pointed up, body wracked with fatigue, tongue poking out. It was all I could do to crawl to a keyboard and type out a note to home.

I began to collect addresses from you guys while I was on the road, so I was able to share my adventures with more and more of you through my Roadkill Reports. For those of you who've read some of them already, you may remember some of the stories about the people I've met along the way, found in the section titled "Traveling Companions," and about a few "Bumps in the Road" that we made it over only by the grace of God. Many of you have written back and blessed me with stories about how you've been blessed by my stories. I often refer to you as my big, happy roadkill family. If you're interested in joining this family, the qualifications aren't that tough: if you're reading this, you're in! Now buckle up for a road trip.

This book is about some of my adventures on the road, whether I was flying, driving, or taking a bus. I've learned so much in the touring life. Most things I've learned the hard way. Some lessons I never want to repeat. I tell the Lord all the time, "Yeah, I got it! I don't want to do that again." I'm learning to keep my head down and my eyes focused on the task at hand and to relax about everything in between.

If life really is one long journey to heaven, then allow me to share with you some of the things I've learned along the way — the hurts, the laughter, the victories, the failings, the crowds, and the loneliness, but mostly the times I've seen God at work. If you've traveled at all — near or far — chances are you'll be nodding your head pretty soon and saying something like, "Don't that beat all! The same thing happened to me up on Bear Wallow Ridge just last Saturday. Didn't it, Martha?" After all, my guess is that we're traveling the same road. And good or bad, maybe this road we're on has been the place God has found for us to serve him.

I handpicked more of my favorite moments, changed the names of some people, and sorted these stories into the categories "Road Weary," about when fatigue threatens to set in on a long journey; "A Bend in the Road," about when life, whether intentionally or by accident, takes a different direction than the one planned; "Enjoy the Ride," about buckling up and hanging on while you live life to its fullest; and finally "Homeward Bound," some encouraging glimpses of a long journey's end.

While writing these stories, and as I dug through my memories and sorted through my notes, I ran over a few little nuggets too short to be complete chapters but spicy enough to keep, so I left them right where I'd run across them, scattered along the way with no real pattern — some here, some there — just like unlucky possums in real life. Count those as you journey through this book, if you like. It beats counting dead hogs (especially since you won't find any in this book).

Now kick back in your favorite chair (I could have said pull up to the table and grab a fork, but I didn't) and enjoy the "roadkill." After all, where I come from, it's legal.

Part 1

Dear Chonda,

I would really like to obtain the DVD that has the song you sang about menopause. You know, the one with the flames of fire leaping upward on the screen?

Chon
123
Any

TRAVELING COMPANIONS

I have found out that there ain't no surer way to find out whether you like people or hate them than to travel with them.

— MARK TWAIN

Come, follow me.

— JESUS OF NAZARETH

I May Be Falling, but I've Got Ahold of Something!

*N*othing's more lonely than traveling by yourself. Conversely, nothing's better than sharing your traveling adventures with a friend, especially when there's pain involved and you need to hold on to something to keep from tipping over.

I had a concert in Buffalo, New York, and my best friend, Alison, was with me. I couldn't wait to take her to see Niagara Falls. Alison has been all over the world—England, Ireland, Italy, France, and Portugal. But she'd never been to Niagara Falls. I had. And so for the day I was her little, obnoxious travel guide.

Alison and I go way back. I got saved 347 times while growing up, and I met Alison at church camp way before I hit the 100 mark. We were about fourteen then. My older sister found her first. They went to Switzerland together on a youth missions trip in the early seventies. After Charlotta was killed in a car accident in 1976, I sort of inherited Alison. For this legacy, I'm forever grateful to my big sister. I wouldn't doubt that she and Alison made some sort of a deal during the friendship. I fancy the idea that the deal was struck in the Swiss Alps: *If anything should happen to me, see to it that my little sister Chonda matches her shoes with her clothes, that she paints her nails once in awhile, and that she doesn't talk with her mouth full—too often.* (They could both be a bit prissy!)

Twenty years ago, I was at the hospital while Alison gave birth to her son, Justin. It was the greatest of nights; it was the saddest of nights (my apologies to Dickens, and David, my literary husband). We'd been together all that day, sensing the time was close. Then later in the evening, sometime before the final and funniest scene of *The Ghost and Mr. Chicken*, Alison went into labor. About thirty-six hours later, Justin was born. About an hour after that, he was rushed by ambulance to another hospital across town—one better equipped to handle his serious lung problems. I stood by Alison when they rolled his little glass house by her bed so she could say goodbye to him before he was taken away. Being there for one another at our points of pain has made our relationship stronger. She is not just my dearest friend; she is my sister. Believe me when I tell you that I'd give her one of David's kidneys if she needed it!

Another time, a terrible migraine headache had Alison laid out on the couch. We were so dirt poor then that a trip to the emergency room was out of the question. Besides, she had an idea: "What I need is just a little pressure on my head. I've done it before, and the throbbing goes away." She looked up at me helplessly from the sofa, tears swimming in her eyes. "Mash my head," she said. So I took a towel and wrapped it as tightly as I could around the top of her head, stuck a pencil in the knot for leverage, and for two hours, I held on and twisted and cranked, Inquisition-like, until my hands and Alison both fell asleep. At least I think she was asleep. Come to think of it, I may have just knocked her out. Either way, her pain was relieved.

I also remember the day I helped Alison pack her belongings and watched as she put her house up for sale and moved eight hours away, closer to her childhood home, because her husband had just walked out and she was left to care for her infant son alone. That point of pain seemed almost unbearable. Her heart was broken, and no towel and pencil could fix this one for her. (I do take credit, though, for praying a man into her life! I will never forget the day that Ken adopted Justin and, of course, married Alison. But I think Alison was just a bonus.)

So I was glad that Alison was there with me at Niagara Falls. "Hurry, hurry!" I called over my shoulder, racing toward the overlook and into the light mist that rolled up out of a rainbow. "They turn it off at six, you know!" She walked faster. She even almost passed me up before her Ph.D. kicked in and she realized that you can't turn off Niagara Falls. We laughed about that for hours. (Okay, I did anyway.)

But as so often happens in real life, our weekend couldn't end like that—with Alison embarrassed and me laughing. Oh no, someone had to get hurt.

The next day we flew down to Omaha, where Dr. Alison soon met with another point of pain when she slipped a disk. She moved through the hotel lobby like a walking question mark. Whenever she stopped, she held on to me to keep from tipping over. This broke my heart. It's so hard to see someone you love in pain. Besides, the moaning and groaning kept me awake all night! I tried to "laugh her better"—you know, tell her jokes to get the endorphins flowing. Science reports every day how the big loads of endorphins produced by laughter have even cured cancer. But Alison was a tough audience. And she'd heard all my jokes. Besides, her back hurt too much for her to laugh.

Alison had tangled with pain a lot over the years. I remembered that she'd had at least two surgeries, some ruptured disks, and a bunch of other yucky things I won't mention. So the slipped disk was not a big surprise. She told me that every so often, something along her spine will shift and leave her crippled for days. This was one of those days.

Thankfully, at the arena where we were staging the Women of Faith conference, one of the volunteers happened to be a massage therapist. So she set up her massage chair, eased Alison into the comfy seat, and began kneading her back and shoulders like biscuit dough, while I shared with the masseuse the art of towel-and-pencil therapy. She promised to try it sometime after we were gone. Alison got a bit of relief from this volunteer, that and a heavy-duty pain pill — then I put her on a plane and pointed her for home, to her doctor-husband. I called ahead and prescribed plenty of TLC, as well as some other doctor stuff that he could do for free, or at least at cost.

I hated to let her go off alone that day, all bent over and shuffling and groaning and even drooling a little bit too. But through my friendship with Alison, I've learned there are many things I can't control. (To that, Dr. Alison would probably say, "Duh!") I can't control Niagara Falls, or Alison's first husband, or even the thin, bony disk in her back that sometimes shifts around to keep her from laughing at my jokes (which I did only to release the endorphins, remember?). And what I have also learned is that no matter what, I pray and I hold on. Every time I do, the love of God always shows up and sweeps over me, picks me up from my island of pain, and carries me off to a place where I can heal. It's better than endorphins.

So when you travel, travel with a friend. Go see Niagara Falls. And when pain shows up to bully you around, just hold on tighter. Hold on to a pencil, a towel, your convictions, to your best friend, to your faith, to the insides of the barrel that takes you over the falls. Hold on tightly, and this pain that bends you into a question mark will pass. You can't hold back God's mercy, and you can't stop Niagara Falls.

ROADKILL REPORT

To Pack the Kitchen Sink or Not?

Do not store up for yourselves treasures on earth ...
But store up for yourselves treasures in heaven.
—MATTHEW 6:19–20

Packing is a science and an art. I think it's time for a new word:
Scienart? Or *artience*?

I'm learning to pack lighter these days because I know that is
the smart thing to do. There were times when I wanted to take
everything—the kitchen sink included—thinking that one day,
out there on the road, I would need it. But all that did was give me
backaches. Although it did make my luggage easier to spot coming
around on that moving belt.

My new dedication to the art of packing took hold when we were
preparing for a ten-day trip to Israel. I've come to realize that no
matter how light you plan to pack, the cause and effect of daily
activities will lead you right back to the kitchen sink. For instance,
David reads a lot and his eyes might get tired, so he'll need his
reading glasses, and a case to protect them, and I'll need a bigger
bag because of the case, and since I have a bigger bag now, I might
as well pack the red shoes for the Thursday evening dinner, and if
we're going to eat out a lot, I might as well bring along the kitchen
sink. See how things grow?

But the best thing you can do is pack light. I try to pack colors
that go with anything, which makes for limitless mix-and-match

combinations. I love reversible clothing. My husband can wear a reversible shirt for four days and never stain it in the same place twice (don't ask). People may think I wear leather pants on stage to make some midlife-crisis statement. Not really. I wear them because they don't wrinkle. And folks might think I wear boots because I'm from Tennessee. But really I wear them because then I don't have to keep my toenails painted, or cut even. I know this all sounds tremendously lazy, but the fact of the matter is I hate to iron and my toenails look better in boots—trust me!

Traveling light is such a powerful concept that Max Lucado even wrote a whole book about it. I bought it in the airport one day—and then had to buy one of those luggage racks on wheels because now my carry-on was too heavy. After about an hour of wheeling it around, spikes of severe pain shot up in my right shoulder and neck, and I nearly missed my flight.

Packing for a trip to the Holy Land can be a bit trickier than packing for a stay in, say, Wisconsin. What to wear to a Christian holy site? A Muslim holy site? A Jewish holy site? Each one is different, so to be safe, we wear layers and wraparounds and things with Velcro and always keep the *Holy Site Dress Code* book handy.

One thing I didn't count on was Lazarus' tomb. It's a small, carved-out cave that barely held us all. But then again, why would you need a roomy tomb? About fifteen of us climbed down into the tomb at the same time. We marveled for a moment at where we were standing and then sang old hymns. We sang one song after another and wept and rejoiced and soaked in the moment. Finally, when someone asked for a Scripture verse, someone else shouted, "Lord, surely by now he stinketh!" Did I mention there's no ventilation in Lazarus' tomb?

Pack light, I remind myself when I go on long trips. And in my day-to-day living, when I try to tote so much baggage around — physical or emotional, real or imagined — I remember that odiferous day in Lazarus' tomb and remind myself that life is short and the tomb at the end of the journey is too small for a kitchen sink.

Although a sink would have been nice, with little soaps and hand towels, maybe a loofah, some hand lotions ...

Chapter 2

My Sweet Harley Momma

When she's at home, Mom likes to watch TV shows like *The Price is Right* and *Walker, Texas Ranger*. She reads those *Reader's Digest* condensed books, and when a bird builds a nest in one of her flowerpots on the back porch, she'll pull up a chair and wait for the eggs to hatch—no matter how long the incubation period. This is my mom's idea of having a good time. So you can imagine my surprise when I took her out on the road with me and she bought herself a brand-new outfit, cleaned out a minibar, and drove out onto the stage in the middle of one of my concerts on a giant Harley-Davidson. When Mom's on the road, she likes to have a really good time.

Now, truth is Mom did all this, but to be fair to her not everything happened on the same night. The new dress came somewhere near Chicago. We waited for our baggage at the claim area, and as usual, mine was one of the last to come out. I grabbed it up and was ready to go when Mom looked both ways along the moving belt, as if it were a street and she were about to cross it.

"I didn't get one," she said.

"You lost your bag?"

"*I* didn't lose it. *They* lost it." And she pointed to the small door draped with strips of plastic where the moving belt took still-unclaimed bags. "I had my best dress in there. I wanted to look nice for you tonight." Her eyes welled up with tears.

"It's okay, Mom." Now the tears began to flow. "They'll find your luggage and send it over to the hotel." More tears. "In the meantime, we'll just go buy you a new dress."

She hiccuped and the tears stopped. "Really?" she said.

So on the way to the hotel, we stopped at the mall, and Mom got her a new, red dress. I think the one she'd lost was a grayish blue—the color of old dishwater.

Mom's bag and the old dress inside made it to the hotel before we did. But that night Mom wore the red dress—before anyone could take it back. When I introduced her like I usually do at a concert, she stood and waved and glowed like a chili pepper.

On another trip, Mom went to Minnesota with me for a weekend. When she comes to my shows with me, I usually like to get her up on stage and have her say a few words, maybe sing a song, and always say a prayer. But we'd been to a couple of other cities before this one, and Mom was tired. So I told her to stay in the room. Relax and watch TV. Take a long, hot bath. Later that night when I got back to the hotel room, Mom seemed to be feeling quite chipper.

"Hello," she said, "how did the night go?" She was eating some chocolate-covered raisins.

I started to tell her about the night when I noticed the candy wrappers on my bed. "Mom, did you eat all these?"

She glanced at the empty wrappers and waved a dismissive hand their way. "Oh, I guess. Much earlier. You've been gone a long time, honey. Lucky for me, the church left this little refrigerator full of all sorts of snacks." She finished the last of the chocolate-covered raisins and struggled with a stubborn Snicker's wrapper.

"Mom, those aren't from the church." I glanced around and found what I was looking for. "And they aren't free."

"No?"

I shook my head and waggled the price guide to the minibar under her nose. "Says here candy bars are three dollars each. How many did you eat?"

She answered, but I couldn't understand her because of the peanuts and caramel. She swallowed. "Well, that makes me feel better then."

"What makes you feel better?"

"Knowing that these snacks don't belong to the church. Because if they did, someone would have some explaining to do."

I didn't understand. She leaned closer and motioned for me to do the same. I smelled something like coconut and nougat on her breath.

"There's liquor in there," she whispered, tipping her head in the direction of the minibar. "They ought to be ashamed." She took a final bite of the Snickers and wasted her best shaming scowl on me. After a dose of this, she raised a hand, palm up, to display the treasure there. Her scowl dissolved. "Kit Kat?" she offered.

But Mom's biggest, wildest time ever out on the road came one night in Chattanooga. Over three thousand women filled the Tivoli Theater in the downtown area, and since Mom only lived a couple hours away, I invited her down and told her to be ready to come up on stage because I wanted to introduce her to everyone.

Just before intermission, I told the audience that my momma was there that night, that I wanted them to make her feel welcome because she'd been ill recently—feeble—and hadn't been able to get out too much.

"Come on up here, Momma," I said.

Just then something that sounded like jet engines exploded back-stage, and I hunkered down and covered my head with the micro-phone, like that would help if the theater roof came crashing down.

But instead of anything crashing down, a steel and chrome beast came rocketing through the backstage curtains—a hog. Or, for those of you not familiar with biker vernacular, a Harley-Davidson. Right there on stage, and in the middle of my concert!

A giant of a man with tattoos on his upper arms and a ponytail swinging behind steered the machine. He wore a black helmet and dark sunglasses and a leather vest. Behind him, holding on for dear life, was . . . *Mom?* She wore a black helmet, shades, and a leather vest too. I think it was the first and only time in my life I've ever been on stage in front of an audience, with a microphone, and couldn't think of a single thing to say. All I could do was laugh and cry. I tried to hurry things up, to get to the bathroom break as quickly as possible.

Mr. Tattoo revved the engine but balanced the bike while I helped Momma off. It took three tries and some heavy lifting to get her right leg up and over the seat. When she had both feet on the ground, Mr. Tattoo drove off and left me with my shaded, leather-adorned motorcycle momma.

She took off her shades in a Fonzie-like fashion and waved to the crowd. I helped her out of her helmet. But she kept the vest on. She liked the vest. Mr. Tattoo had to ask for it back later.

There's something about the road that makes my momma want to live it up—to dress in bright colors, to raid the chocolate caches of this country, to accessorize with leather. Maybe it's because she recognized long ago (after losing two of her own beautiful daughters so tragically) that our journey here is a short one, and you've got to "seize the day" (that *carpe*-Latin thing, you know). Or maybe it's only because when she's on the road with me, she can never find *The Price Is Right* in the hotel room. Whichever, all I know is that when I say, "Mom, do you want to go with me this weekend?" she'll pack up her little suitcase (the one that won't hold nearly all the things she'll need) and meet me at the bus early.

Mom is that traveling companion who will never allow the journey to grow long or dull. Every day for her is an adventure, and every mile I travel with her is an adventure for me! With Mom tagging along, if you ask, "Are we there yet?" it won't be because you're bored. She's learned what many of us take so long to realize: we're moving at a pretty fast clip, and those mile markers sometimes zip by way too fast for us to read them. If God's mercies are indeed new every morning (and they are), then we have to be constantly paying attention and seizing all the goodness that comes our way. When you put Momma on a moving bus with a kitchen full of snacks and a satellite dish that can lock in on *The Price Is Right* just about any hour of the day, she will *carpe diem*!

That's the phrase I was looking for! I think I even know what that means: I need a new dress.

ROADKILL REPORT

Who's Driving This Bus Anyway?

I said, "Oh, that I had the wings of a dove!
I would fly away and be at rest."
—PSALM 55:6

Last night I got a pretty good scare on the bus. At first I thought I
was dreaming — so that would make it a nightmare, wouldn't it? But
then when I realized I was awake, I wished it were only a nightmare.

I could tell it was before sunrise, because just enough light was
coming through the windows that I could see my way around without
bumping into everything. I crawled out of my bunk and shuffled
off to the bathroom. That's when I noticed George, our bus driver,
making himself a fresh cup of coffee.

"Good morning, George," I said sleepily.

"Good morning, Chonda," he said, tearing open a sugar packet
and dumping its contents into a cup of blackness.

I reached for the door just as the bus swerved a little. *We're
moving?* But George was right there. I could reach out and touch him
if I wanted. I'm dreaming, that's it, I thought. I wondered if I could
fly. I tried to will myself to fly around the bus, just for kicks. That
would be fun (more fun than wasting a good dream on shuffling to
the bathroom!). But I couldn't. Just then the bus hit a pothole, and
the jolt shot up through my bad knee. (Not dreaming!) "George?" I
said, very much awake now. "Are we moving?" I looked to the front
of the bus, but the heavy drape that separated the cab from the

back was pulled to, so I couldn't see anything. "And you're standing there?"

George looked up from his coffee cup and made a little gasping sound. "Oh, you caught me," he said. He turned and tiptoed toward the front of the bus, as if he were hurrying back before he got into anymore trouble.

Before I had time to panic, George suddenly stopped and turned around. He grinned. "I'm just kidding. Chad has his license too," he told me. Chad was part of the crew. "He's just giving me a short break."

I exhaled. And even though I didn't think his little joke was all that funny, I chuckled politely, for George's sake.

When I came out of the bathroom, George was back behind the wheel. I could see his elbow through an opening in the drape. I shuffled slowly back to the bunk, noticing that Chad was nowhere in sight. Did Chad really have his license? Had he really relieved George for a spell? Had he really been on the other side of that drapery? Was I really awake? I tried to fly back to my bunk and whacked my bad knee on the door casing. Oh yeah, I was definitely awake. But that was all I really knew for sure.

Chapter 3

Traveling with Royalty

*T*he bus rolled into Rochester, New York, early one morning with me and my traveling companion for about the last three months, Sandi Patty, onboard. So we did what I think anyone who's not from New York would do in that same situation: we practiced our Brooklyn accents. I knew we were a long way from Brooklyn, but I figured the good people of Rochester would come closer to accepting me and getting my jokes if they could understand me. Sandi was so much better at it than me, but I had to keep in mind that she'd been to Carnegie Hall before, and I'm sure she had to order food when she was there—in the city—talk to the doorman, and maybe even hail a cab. Not to mention that she's from just north of Indianapolis. She was more familiar with the language than I was. So with her help, "I do declare, I'd love a nice helpin' of some grits" became "Yo, me and the girls are hungry here—What'cha got?" The more we practiced, the funnier I got, at least to me anyway. Sometimes it's fun to pretend to be something you're not.

We were performing at the Theater on the Ridge. It's at the Kodak plant—the place where they invented pictures. We ate lunch in the employees' cafeteria and then snooped around the old building while no one was around to stop us. Every kind of camera you could think of was on display, as long as it was a Kodak. And along with the cameras were dozens of photographs that'd been taken with them. They say the camera doesn't lie. So here were dozens of people frozen in their moments of truth, captured with smiles, frowns, scowls, food in their mouths, hair coifed, hair mussed, fine threads, tattered threads, bare feet, and shiny shoes. Yep, pretty honest.

I've got a few of those superhonest pictures myself, but I keep them where no one can see them, tucked away in a brain wrinkle that no one will ever find. I keep them for a couple of reasons: one, to remind me of who I am, and two, to remind me that I need reminding of who I am. Know what I'm talking about? (Nod, nod.)

I had been in Rochester not too long before this trip, when the Women of Faith Conference had rolled through town. I've worked with this group for many years. If you're not familiar with them, I can tell you some pretty big names pass across their stage: singers, authors, speakers. People with more books and CDs than a Mark Lowry yard sale (had to do that!). Anyway, I can remember hanging out backstage like a wallflower, concerned about more than just my accent. These people were mini-gods! I went through months and months of "comparison shopping." They have suits; I have leather pants. They have outlines; I have punch lines. They have degrees and pedigrees; I have a mutt.

So I did what most comedians do when they believe no one thinks they're funny: I moped and walked around with my shoulders hunched over. Come to find out, though, I wasn't seeing the real picture. All that moping was just *me* worrying about *me*. Before long, people I didn't know all that well were telling me jokes — *my own jokes!* When you're a comedian and people repeat your jokes back to you, it's usually a good sign that they liked the joke and thought you were funny, and now they want to tell you your own joke and laugh along with you. (Ask any comedian, besides me, and she'll tell you that. Then, just for fun, repeat one of her jokes back to her.) After only a few of these conferences, at which I was so worried about fitting in, it seemed everyone in the green room had turned into a Southern preacher's daughter who got saved 347 times growing up. I was blown away — by their acceptance of me as I was and by the fact that people from up North sound funny when they try to talk Southern.

I've been reading a lot about the apostle Paul lately. One of the things I love about Paul is his "roadkill reports." When Paul saw an injustice, when he was aggravated about something, he'd fire off a letter (many times railing against a whole town). When he was tired, you knew it. When he was discouraged, you knew it. He was honest enough to say, "I fail. I constantly do what I know I shouldn't do." He was a pretty "real" kind of guy who could still inspire us from the floor of a prison cell. He also lamented about "a thorn in his flesh," which he finally became grateful for because he recognized that it was that very thing that kept him "prayed up" and leaning into his relationship with God. You know what I think? I think that just maybe the thorn in his flesh was his *flesh*! I know that it's *me* that keeps *me* working to know God better because no one knows *me* like I do!

And as long as we're being honest, I really do shop at Wal-Mart. I know that's part of a joke I tell (and people will often tell it back to me), but it's all true. I like to hit 'em in every state. At a Wal-Mart in Missouri, a woman stopped me and said, "Oh my. Are you Chonda Pierce?" I smiled and nodded. "I thought I recognized that voice," she said. I stopped smiling and kept nodding. "I am shocked you would shop at Wal-Mart. You should be at Saks Fifth Avenue!" I just laughed and told her about the big sale in aisle nine. You should have seen her scurry away. On the way to my car, a young woman who used to work for me said, "You know you should be careful." I said,

"Oh, privacy is no big deal out here." She said, "I'm not talking about your privacy. You may not want to shop in such common places." And she waved a dismissive hand over one of my Wal-Marts. "You have an image to keep up, you know?" (You'll notice I said she *used* to work for me!)

Now, I know that if I didn't have my face plastered on half a dozen videos out there, I wouldn't have your attention. Right now, though, it seems I have a platform (a soapbox, some say). So while you're here, let me admit that even though I'm comfortable, there are still many things I want to do. There are shows I want to write and perform and books in my head I want to get down on paper. There are towns I'd like to visit and places I dream of seeing and long to be a part of. Therefore, the bus keeps rolling on. Already on this journey, I've been honored with a couple of trophies and some gold records. But I also know that I am a size eight-and-climbing (up from a six-and-climbing) and am forty-five years old. There's not enough Oil of Olay in the world to keep my face in demand forever! But I'm here today to see where this bus goes.

I still have days when I need to "get over myself." But I can tell you this: there's no image here. I have "ticked" days and I have china days! Who knows? Maybe if I had paid more attention to my image, I'd have a sitcom on TV by now. Maybe if I had worried about what "everyone" thinks, I'd have gotten more facials. Truth is, all the hype about me is just not me. I may never be on *Oprah*. I may never write a life-changing, didactic concordance to the book of Ephesians (whatever that is). I may speak my mind one too many times and never get played on the radio again. I might not be all that funny, and I may never loose these extra fifteen pounds on my hips. But today — *today* — I'm comfortable with who I am.

I know this is a tender subject — accepting yourself, being happy with yourself, blooming where you are planted (that's the one, when

I'm at my lowest, that sets me off like a car alarm). Accepting our-selves is a hurdle we sometimes have to leap over again and again. But we're women, and women love to comparison shop, don't we? I wish I could sing like Sandi Patty. I wish I were as smart as all those Women of Faith speakers (or at least the special guests). I wish I were as skinny as Philip Yancey.

Have you ever been guilty of thinking that the ultimate accep-tance lies somewhere other than in Christ? I see that hand, and that hand, and that hand, and ... Seems we live in a world of icons and accolades. We look for affirmation from a gazillion different places —from Mom's hug to a plaque that claims we're Employee of the Month. We want to be recognized and rejoiced over. We fancy that if only someone the world says is great would notice us, it would be the same as having our purple veins flow with royal blood. But listen: as long as you have a relationship with the Lord Jesus Christ, your blood is *already* royal! Employee of the Month for Life can't touch that!

I finally gave up on the fake accent when the locals kept saying, "Excuse me, but what did you say?" And that night in Rochester, New York, a roomful of people seemed happy to let me simply be me. So instead of hearing us mangle their language, they heard some incredible singing from my traveling companion, Sandi Patty—sing-ing that rattled the rafters and shook the Kodak photographs hang-ing on the walls (in a good way). They heard my funny stories and repeated them to me later that night in the lobby as we personally greeted our guests and waved them off. That night they saw a couple of forty-something gals who are larger than a size two do what they do, and do it as honestly as they could: Love Jesus Christ right out loud. Bloom where we are planted.

And that was as real as we could possibly get. I wonder if anyone took a picture?

Chapter 4

Are We There Yet?

I love to travel with my kids. And if you have kids and can't understand this, trust me, once they get out of diapers and car seats and you no longer need the stroller, the crate of cleaning supplies, and the bag of snacks, you'll see that traveling with your kids can be fun. Mine always find a way to surprise me. Just when I'm ready to ground them for life, they do something that makes them look like a pair of angels. And just when I think they are a pair of angels, they do something that makes me want to ground them for life. For instance, there was that time we took them to the Holy Land with us ...

But first let me tell you a bit about my children, about something that happened just recently. I was in San Jose—*without* my kids—and it was Mother's Day. (I know, I know: I'm a terrible mother!) But I'd found my way to San Jose for a big Women of Faith conference and then couldn't find my way out. (Those of you who were born before 1970 or who listen to the oldies station will get that one.)

Anyway, so there I was two thousand miles away from my wonderful children on Mother's Day morning. I'd missed the big breakfast-in-bed ritual that takes place every Mother's Day at my house. Maybe you know what I'm talking about: A bowl of cornflakes is served on a cookie sheet draped with a dishtowel, with a flower from the garden angled between the cereal bowl and the orange Kool-Aid (which the children still argue is the same thing as orange juice). A beetle of some sort drops from the flower and burrows into the square of butter meant for the toast. And, totally unsupervised by their father but receiving his full blessing, they carve a slice of bologna into the shape of a heart and fry it for me, because they know that's what I made for *my* mom when I was a little girl. And then there's the card. Only, since the crowd at the card section is so large and unruly the day before Mother's Day (especially those last few minutes before the store closes on the eve of Mother's Day, when the cards are marked down half-price), my children will purchase something from the other end of the aisle, like a "Congratulations on Your New House!" card or a "You Deserve That Promotion" card. Then they'll scratch out the words that don't apply (usually most of them) and pencil in the words that do. At least it'll come with a matching envelope.

That's Chera and Zachary. My resourceful children.

Speaking of resourceful, let me tell you one more story about my children, and then I'll make my point for this chapter — about traveling with the kids — I promise. Not long ago, they started their own company, called Stacks of Wax. They made candles and sold them. They even built a website by themselves and took pictures of their creations and carried flyers all over the neighborhood to advertise. Now, there's not much to making a candle: melt some wax and pour it around a string. It's all the melting-the-wax stuff I could have done without. When I'd come home from the road, I could tell just how busy Stacks of Wax had been the last couple of days by how far me and my luggage would skate across the room. You see, every time wax gets cooked, a slick, waxy film settles onto everything close by — until the next big bologna fry. Then the whole place goes into meltdown.

I was thinking about pulling the plug on the whole waxy operation (right after I skated into the refrigerator and scattered magnets all over the lower half of the house), when one day I walked upstairs—where the packing and shipping department was located —and I found them wrestling with supersticky packing tape and some boxes packed with freshly made candles. Three money envelopes lay on the floor beside them, each clearly marked: *Profits, Parts,* and *Tithes.*

When they think I'm not looking, they can be little angels.

But when they think I'm nearby, they'll do something like spill wax on the stove burners and set off all the smoke detectors.

Now for that traveling story ...

Not long ago, my husband, David, and I took the children with us to Israel. Chera had just finished her second year in college and Zachary his first in high school, so they were old enough to understand all the talk of battles and skirmishes that had taken place either thousands of years ago or only fifteen minutes before. Israel is a place of such extreme contrasts: the location of the greatest display of love and sacrifice ever and the location of the greatest display of pain and hatred ever. Nearly everywhere we went, we could find a sign—usually next to a basilica—that read something like "Site of the famous Battle of _____."

"Wow," Zachary said, "church over is here is a lot like church back home, huh?" (I told you Zach is old enough to know some things.)

There's so much history to try to wrap your mind around in Israel, so many stones everywhere you go, and each one must tell a story. And that's how our children learned a lot about Israel, by bringing home some of the stones. (I hope that was legal. If not, oops!) We wanted the stones to go into our fireplace hearth. Over the years, we've collected bits of rock from all over the world—from the tops of mountains, from the depths of canyons, from rivers and seas and volcanoes. As we traveled all over Israel, it was fun to watch Zach and Chera (and sometimes David) collect nuggets of Bible history. Up in the northern part of Israel, in the shadow of Mount Hermon, Zachary pocketed a smooth, round stone and grinned and said, "Maybe this one killed Goliath." At the Sea of Galilee, David did the same and said, "Maybe this is one Peter tossed into the water when the fishing was bad." Chera found one in Jerusalem and said, "Maybe this is the one Jesus kicked through the streets when he was a kid, coming in for the Feast of the Tabernacles."

Now we have a basketful of stones waiting to be glued into the hearth, each one a lesson about our God and the time and place he chose to come down and love us.

Not long after we returned from Israel, my children surprised me one day with an emailed picture when I was off traveling again. They wanted to show how much they'd come to understand about the Holy Land. Their father had snapped the picture, so it was new to me. In this shot, they are wearing long, flowing white robes and look like a pair of angels as they wait to be baptized in the Jordan River—except that they are locked in a death hug as they roll on the ground! Zach has Chera in a choke hold, and Chera's fist is poised just above Zach's noggin. They're in the midst of a "real" Tennessee knock-down-drag-out. (I have to make it clear that this picture was staged just as a joke for their comedian mom. I still remember all the mail I got about the cat joke I made twelve years ago.) This wasn't exactly the lesson I was hoping they would take away from the Holy Land. But I must say, the deep green of the Jordan River contrasted with their billowy white baptismal gowns and Chera's blood-red face, from oxygen deprivation, was so inspiring that I quickly turned the scene into my laptop screen saver.

Yes, I love to travel with my kids and to see them experience things for the first time. But the greatest part is when they teach me something new about a world I've lived in for forty-something years. With Chera and Zachary along, jobs become projects, necessary tasks become missions, and simple stones become lessons about God's love. Our children's eyes are focused differently than our own. Stand next to them by a blooming rose bush sometime, and while you take in the burst of a velvet red bud, they'll find the Japanese beetle crawling on the underside of a clump of leaves down near the bottom, in the back. Watch the clouds together long enough and soon they'll see a dragon or a flying cat. Take them to the Holy Land and pick up a stone and share with them that it's highly possible that Jesus handled that very one, and maybe one of them will say something like, "Touched it? Come on, guys, he *made* every one of these. Duh!" Like Zachary said on the banks of the Galilee.

Yeah, when I'm not stuck in San Jose and my children aren't busy melting wax to make candles, I love to travel with them, whether it's halfway around the world or just down to the store for ice cream. Is there a better way to see the world than through the eyes of your children?

ROADKILL REPORT

It's a Hard-Rock Life

I remember you in my prayers.
—ROMANS 1:9–10

A bus is like a box of chocolates: you never know what you're going to get.

I don't own a tour bus, for many reasons. One, they're too big and I don't have any place to keep one. Two, they cost too much to use for only four months out of the year. And three, they cost too much when they break down.

So when I need a bus, I lease one from a bus-leasing company. Then all I'm required to do is ride from one place to another and concentrate on my punch lines, not hydraulic seals. Sometimes when the rock stars aren't working, they lease their buses out—to take the edge off storage costs, I guess. One weekend we got a plush ride, and we knew it. Tan leather sofas, state-of-the-art sound system, DVD players in every bunk, a lighted shower that would change colors for no apparent reason. And one of the coolest things this bus had was a giant flat-screen plasma TV that was hidden behind a painting of a forest. Just push a button and the painting would slide down to reveal the screen. Pretty cool.

The first thing the bus driver said to me when he pulled up at my front door was not hello, or good to meet you, or what kind of work is it you do? He told me this bus belonged to a big rock-and-roll star. One that I'd heard of and seen on TV, but just so we don't get into any legal trouble, I'll call him Wild-Man Party-Animal Living-for-the-Moment Mr. Rock 'n' Roll, or Mr. Rock 'n' Roll for short.

So before heading out, we blessed the bus. And we thought we had that wildness taken care of for now. That is, until we tried to watch a little TV. The bus was so plush it even had TiVo on board. TiVo is like a computer for your TV set. You can record whatever's on the screen and play it back later so you don't miss anything, whether it's *Bambi* or "Bambi," if you know what I mean.

This particular weekend my ladies' small group was traveling with me to Memphis. Somewhere around Jackson, Tennessee, someone hit the play button on the TiVo, and for about five whole seconds, I feared our eyeballs would burn out because of what we saw, because that's how long it took me to dive from Mr. Rock 'n' Roll's kitchenette to the controls of his big-screen TV. I hit the right button the first time and the TV went blank, and so did the faces of my ladies' small group.

Above the hum of the bus tires on Interstate 40, I said, "Let us pray." And together we reblessed the bus and the TV and decided to listen to music instead.

We might have survived the night just fine after that, but Momma, who actually draped a tablecloth over our TV set until I was a teenager, couldn't wait to show her Internet chat room devotion group what the inside of a real tour bus looks like.

She guided them from the steering wheel, past the nine bunks with their own flip-down screens, to the rainbow-lighted shower, to the spacious back bunk. They were bug-eyed the whole time. My guess is they'd never seen the likes of this in a house, let alone in a bus! And then Mom had to show them the fancy TV behind the disappearing painting. "And that painting disappears, and there's a TV behind it," she told them.

"No!"

"Yes! Watch this." She pushed a button and the forest fell and the TV blinked to life, and there was "Bambi," right where she'd left off earlier. None of the buttons seemed to work for Mom now, so in desperation, she sort of flung herself at the screen and covered what she could with arms and hands and torso and sweater. "Help! Someone help me!"

Had the bus driver not been close by, my little mom might have punched out "Bambi."

Well, this certainly gave them something to chat about in the chat room for the next week.

We had a real shock that night, but it wasn't like Mr. Rock 'n' Roll had set us in his sights. After that night, however, we've definitely got him in our sights—me, my ladies' small group, Mom, and the entire Senior Citizens Devotional Chat Room. We prayed for Mr. Rock 'n' Roll that night. And we make it a point to say a prayer for him every time we hear his name.

Not long ago, Mr. Rock 'n' Roll was arrested for punching out a DJ in a strip club. The reporter was kind of jokey about the whole thing. But I couldn't help but say a prayer for him. On the news that night, the singer shook the hair out of his eyes because his hands were cuffed behind him. He smiled for the camera, but what I saw, when his face covered the screen, was a man in trouble, crying out, "Help me! Someone help me!"

We're trying, me and my ladies' small group.

It's easy to beat up on someone who hurts you, or embarrasses you, or simply doesn't believe like you do. What's hard is praying a sincere prayer that the person's heart will soften—even if he is Mr. Rock 'n' Roll. Especially if he is Mr. Rock 'n' Roll.

Part 2

Dear Chonda,

We had a great time at your concert in Pittsburgh last night. I am a breast-cancer survivor of twelve years, so I could really relate to your mom's story about her cancer. After my surgery when I was going through chemo, my bedtime routine included taking off my wig, taking out my contact lenses, and removing my prosthesis. I used to say to my husband, "When I get to a part you want, let me know, and I'll throw it over to you."

Chon
123
Any

ce
Lane
USA

BUMPS IN THE ROAD

Man always travels along precipices.
His truest obligation is to keep his balance.
—POPE JOHN PAUL II

It was much pleasanter at home,
when one wasn't always
growing larger and smaller,
and being ordered about
by mice and rabbits.
—ALICE, IN *ALICE IN WONDERLAND*

Chapter 5

Somebody Say Something

*N*ot long ago I was in Oklahoma. I can never hear *Oklahoma* without spelling it (O-k-l-a-h-o-m-a), or say it without putting an exclamation mark at the end: Oklahoma! Or write it without using italics: *Oklahoma!* Or say it without adding "OK" to the very end. Here's how I handle Oklahoma: O-k-l-a-h-o-m-a. *Oklahoma!* OK. There. I did it. Also, when I think of Oklahoma, I think of trouble, and I think about how one skinny cowboy saved the day with just two tiny words.

Even though I never got to the actual state until many years later, my Oklahoma story takes place in high school. You see, my senior year in high school, we put on a musical. You guessed it: *Oklahoma!* Mrs. Mayo was my drama teacher: short, stout, and gifted with unbelievable projection abilities. She cast me as Laurey, who has lots of singing parts and even a kissing scene. (This was unheard of at the high school level at that time. But Mrs. Mayo and I talked it over and agreed the scene was absolutely necessary for the proper artistic angst to be delivered to our targeted audience.)

If you're not familiar with the play, let me tell you briefly that about halfway through, there is a dream sequence featuring Laurey and her beau, Curly, who dance almost ballet-style — how else but in a dream can you have classical dance in a play about ranchers and cowboys? My little sister, Cheralyn, played Laurey in the dream. She was graceful and svelte and sort of looked like me. This play also has a cadre of cowboys who don't do much more than walk around bowlegged or stand around bowlegged, with their thumbs in their belt loops, and try to look interested (when they aren't singing songs about cattle). My future husband, David, was one of these cowboys.

For seven shows, we all played our parts and very little went wrong. Then during show eight, all our hard work might have been erased if it were not for one lone cowboy who proved to be quick on his bowlegged feet — David, my future husband.

But first, another brief synopsis: this play also has an auction scene. A grandmotherly character holds a pie auction (like they used to do in the olden days in Oklahoma, I guess). The young gent who buys a pie gets a date with the girl who made it. Curly bids on Laurey's pie because that's the way young love is moving and the audience wants them to get together because they are just so cute together. But the evil Judd steps in and outbids Curly (boo, hiss, boo). Judd's winning bid is supposed to be ten bits. So you see, there's a lot of bidding back and forth before that — you know, to build up the tension like you do in any good story.

So for seven shows we did this: cowboys bid, tension builds, Curly gets snubbed, and Judd gets Laurey (boo, hiss, boo). But on the eighth night, when grandma started the auction, someone bid one bit and then there was silence. Nothing. Tension began to build too soon and at the wrong time. Grandma scanned the crowd. She raised her eyebrows. She pursed her lips. "Do I hear two bits?" she said. No one said a word. More unwanted tension. Cowboys looked at their boots. Ranchers looked off to their fields. "I said, do I hear two bits?" Grandma craned her neck stage left and stage right. Curly was patiently waiting to toss in his eight bits. Judd was waiting to top him with ten bits. No one knew what had happened to the two-bit guy. At this point the auction, the play, all of life, had ground to a halt awaiting the offering of two bits.

So in stepped David (bowlegged, of course). He scratched his throat, the way cowboys do when they haven't shaved in weeks. He pointed his chin upward, like he might spit the words across the room rather than say them. With all the intonation and inflection and import and even dialect anyone could ever put into two little words, David said, "Two bits."

Immediately someone said four-bits, someone else said six. Curly said eight, Judd bid ten and got the girl (boo, hiss, boo). The rest of the play played out without a single hitch. We even did two more shows, and the two-bit man (whoever he was) delivered his lines flawlessly on those two nights. For nine shows, David was just another cowboy, chewing on a straw, holding up his pants with his thumbs. But on that one special night, he saved the show.

Or at least that's how David tells the story to our children, at least once a year and absolutely every single time we ever travel to Oklahoma —I mean, O-k-l-a-h-o-m-a. *Oklahoma!* OK.

Before our first rehearsal, Mrs. Mayo made sure we each had a script. And we had rehearsed—oh, how we had rehearsed. We even had seven great performances under our big cowboy belt buckles when we hit that big bump. But something had still gone wrong. Even so, seems all we needed to get through was a little push, a nudge, someone to lend us a couple of words that would get us over the gap that had brought an entire production to a halt.

What's scary is that if gaps can open up when you're working with a script and a director and endless rehearsals, when you are as prepared as we were, it's not surprising that they can break open when you're motoring along at this breakneck speed we call life. Someone once said, "Want to make God laugh? Tell him your plans." So what do you do when the road that you thought was the right one comes to an end? When there's a gap? A barrier? A detour sign? A bump in the road?

When that happens to me today, I don't hesitate to look in God's direction, sometimes raising my eyebrows, sometimes craning my neck to the right and to the left, searching the heavens, sometimes dropping to my knees, and I wait and listen for God to drop in his "two bits" worth, no matter how long and awkward the silence. Only then, once I have those words of direction from God, do I feel it's okay to keep traveling on.

And that's what I think of every time I travel to O-k-l-a-h-o-m-a. *Oklahoma!* OK.

Chapter 6

A Pig in a Blanket

*T*he bus pulled into Bristol, Tennessee, early in the morning. I could smell the Smoky Mountains from my bunk. Twelve people were on the bus, and we were just starting a brand-new tour called "Be Afraid, Be Very Afraid." I wasn't so sure about the other eleven people on the bus, but I was a bit afraid.

I had my jokes; I had my stories and songs. But we had not rehearsed even once as a team. But after all, it's only little ol' me up there with a microphone, right? And if something goes wrong, I could just make a joke out of it, right? That's what's great about being a comedian: everything's a part of the act. But the other thing about being a comedian is timing. If the timing is good, there's real potential for great comedy. If the timing is bad, watch out for disaster.

Bristol, Tennessee, is home to one of the biggest NASCAR races every year, so they've seen their share of car crashes. But on this night, they were about to witness one whopper of a train wreck.

Five thousand people, mostly women, came out to see our new show that night. And you don't have to be a math whiz to know that five thousand women divided by four bathrooms means — okay, so maybe you need *some* math skills. I know you can't rehearse potty breaks, but someone should have thought to call the Port-O-Potty people, or at least made up some signs that said, "I know this is a men's room, but tonight we need it more. Good luck," and posted them on every men's room door in the place.

And because the room was so big, which meant I was so far away, we brought in this fancy piece of technology called an IMAG. Basically, it's a couple of cameras and some big screens so that people in the back row can see up my nostrils. "Back it up there, buddy," I told the cameraman at one point. "All those chins will scare the children!"

As the night went on, I made jokes about the bathroom line. I made jokes about my nose and my chins and the spinach stuck in my teeth. Up to this point, I'd been able to smooth over every little glitch in an unrehearsed night with a slick veneer of comedy. But I don't think even Bob Hope could have smoothed over a human pig in a blanket wriggling upright behind me and slowly moving from stage left to stage right—all while I'm trying to sing about heaven. Let me explain.

You see, when you start to plan one of these tours, you have lots of meetings. In these meetings, you decide things like what kind of lights to use, how many, the kind and number of speakers, who will make phone calls, who will promote the tour. Just about everything you can think of (with the exception of that Port-O-Potty call) gets taken care of. We even talked for a long time about what the set will look like—you know, should flowers be on the front of the stage or the back, on a stool or a chair, in a vase? Or maybe a sculpture that looks like a thyroid gland (well, it did to me anyway, and that's why I voted no). So sometime during the meeting someone said, "Hey, I've got an idea! Since the theme of the night is all about overcoming fear, let's do something to demonstrate a change. A before and after."

"You mean like put on makeup during the show?" I think I said.

"That would work, but I'm thinking of something even more dramatic. Let's do something with the backdrop."

Right here is where I probably should have said, "Whoa!" or even "No!" At the very least I should have said, "Only if we can rehearse one hundred times and not a single time less." But instead I said, "What do you have in mind? A backdrop?"

"How about two?"

Okay, I was hooked. I listened to his story.

"Let's have a backdrop of an old building. Something classical, with columns and Roman architecture. Only the building is old and cracked. Vines are climbing up in unkempt fashion. Windows are broken. The only thing missing is a "Condemned" sign on the front. Then at the end, as you sing this song about changing and being made complete, the backdrop literally peals away to reveal a beautiful, pristine, completely restored mansion. It'll be just like stepping into heaven!"

I thought on this for a bit. I had a vision in my head. (And I was hearing trumpets and strings and harp music at the same time.) "We can do that?" I asked.

"Are you kidding? We got IMAG, which will zoom right in on your back sinuses. We got portable potties to serve thousands at once, which reminds me, I need to make a phone call. But first, what about the backdrop? Are you ready for transformation? A metamorphosis?"

"So how do we pull the backdrop? Make the change?"

"You leave that to me. If that's a yes, I'll get busy on the design. I know just who to call." He started scratching around on his desktop for a phone number, so the meeting was over and we all broke to leave. "Hey —" he called and stopped us all. "Can someone get me the number of the Port-O-Potty people?"

And so the pieces of the tour were found and collected and brought to the bus to be loaded. Rehearsal opportunities came and went. But after all, this was a comedy show. It wasn't like I had a band and we all needed to make sure we were in the same key and all, was it?

When we set up in Bristol, everything seemed to go smoothly. Lights, IMAGs, a stool, my microphone, my bottle of water. Not too bad. Even the backdrops looked nice. It was just as we'd planned. The front backdrop was a mansion in ruins, almost life-size. It was about fifteen feet high and forty feet long. The painted-on columns looked as if they'd crumble at any instant. The mansion on the second backdrop, the one in the back, was indeed heavenly. It almost sparkled, and who wouldn't want to live there?

"Okay," I asked. "So how do we make the switch? How do we get from ruins to heaven?"

"Well," my hi-tech guy said, rubbing his chin thoughtfully. "Because it's so big, I've got this idea that won't require pulleys and wenches."

"Weights and counterweights then?"

He shook his head.

"Pneumatic actuators?"

He shook his head.

"What then?"

"Velcro."

"What?"

"We've got a long strip of Velcro all the way along the top. When you hit that bridge and go into that final chorus—the one that even *sounds* like heaven—Gordon will slip out and grab hold of one corner and peel it back like this." He pulled slightly on one corner to demonstrate how easily it could be done. "It's like turning a page, which, I think, will be even more dramatic. Pretty clever, I think."

"Have we practiced this yet?"

He bit his lip. "Not really. It's just so big, and we didn't have room ... but it just peels right off and *voilà!* Heaven!" He pointed to the backdrop with both hands, palms up, like one of those girls on *The Price Is Right* pointing to a box of Kraft macaroni.

And so the show went on. Five thousand of us laughed and cried. We took an extra-long potty break. We talked about what was on my nose and in my teeth. And when I got to the last song, I sang my heart out. I felt the Spirit move, and we seemed to teeter on the edge of heaven. What a great night it had turned out to be. What an incredible crowd. They laughed when they were supposed to and cried when I cried. And when I sang about heaven, they stood and applauded, not me, I don't think—but God and the whole idea of heaven and the room in the mansion he has gone ahead to prepare for us. When I peeked back, I got a glimpse of our dazzling mansion, rippling the way cloth will when a breeze passes by. So I guess it did work. Like he said: *voilà!*

As I stepped off the stage, Alison, my best friend in the world who travels with me quite a bit, was there to meet me and help me down the dark steps. "How did it all look?" I asked.

"We'll talk about it on the bus," she said. And she led me (tugged me) all the way there.

While I waited on the bus for the crew, someone brought me a videotape of the night's show, and we fast-forwarded it to the end. Everyone wanted me to see this. I couldn't wait. Someone pushed play, and there I was (I've got to go on a diet!). The colors looked nice—"popped!" is how we say it in the business. Oh, and I loved the ferns at the front of the stage. That was definitely a good call. As I sang to the bridge of the song, I saw Gordon, dressed in black like a ninja, walk onto the stage behind me. I thought he was supposed to "slip," not walk. I kept singing. He gave the big sheet a tug, and it began to peel back, just like the plan I'd heard. Then something up high, out of sight, seemed to stick. So Gordon did what anyone else probably would have done: he tugged harder.

Now, the funny thing about Velcro is that there is no speed control. If you could look closely at Velcro, like under a microscope, you'd see thousands of teeny-tiny hooks latching onto thousands of teeny-tiny rings. It doesn't take much to pull one of those out. It takes a pretty good tug to pull thousands out at a time. It looked to me like Gordon gave it a pretty good tug. Yards of Velcro broke loose at once. Yards of backdrop fell way too fast. So Gordon did what most anyone would have done in that moment: he started raking in the falling cloth as fast as he possibly could. The painted-on columns fell, and Gordon caught them like Samson and wrapped them about his body. He turned artfully to make room for the next column, and the next, and the next. (Think Tim Conway trying to break free of flypaper in the background while Carol Burnett sings a serious ballad.)

At the key change, and with my hands raised and eyes closed and turned to heaven, Gordon, completely mummified by now, baby-stepped it to the edge of the stage and disappeared into the shadows. I noticed on the video that that was the time I happened to glance back to see the pristine, life-size mansion still rippling behind me. This part looked nice.

The bus was pretty quiet as we soaked all of this in. No one even laid a finger on the snacks. Before long, the crew began to load up, and still no one uttered a word about the mummy, the cocoon, the taco, the burrito, the pig in a blanket (and all the other names we would come up with later). But when Gordon came aboard, I asked him, "What in the world happened with the backdrop?"

Everyone fell silent. Gordon scanned the room. He appeared shocked. His eyes widened, and he said, "You could see me?"

We made some serious changes after that night. One, we had bathroom signs printed up. And two, Velcro was out for live performances. I know the tour was about fear and how we can't be ruled by fear, but the prospect of seeing Gordon wrapped as snug as a bug in a rug night after night terrified me.

Funny thing is I'm not sure anyone in the audience even realized what was going on. We were too busy worshiping. Maybe the people had been like me, their eyes turned up and focused on heaven. Maybe all they'd noticed, like me, was the image of that final mansion, rippling in the wake of the Gordon breeze. Or maybe they'd seen everything, even the hairs on the back of Gordon's hands (like I noticed on the video), but heaven's too big to be shaken by a man caught up in fabric. Haven't we all seen worse?

I never got even one letter or email asking what in the name of everything decent and kind was the ninja in the sheet all about? And believe me, I get letters asking about weirder things than that. I guess the truth is that sometimes we pay far more attention to our screw-ups than those around us do. And other times, when we hit a bump in the road, we'll wrap ourselves up in our troubles like a cocoon and then pray no can see us. The reality is that God's there in both instances, and in neither instance will he beat us up or rewind the video to remind us of our low points. We do a good job of that on our own. Ain't it good to know that God will always use our best efforts in spite of ourselves—and in spite of unpredictable Velcro?

As we loaded up and moved away from the mountains, that wonderful mountain air that I'd wakened with earlier gave way to the aroma of twelve people on a bus. Oh boy, and the tour had just begun.

ROADKILL REPORT

I Think I Broke My Foot

Sing joyfully to the Lord, you righteous;
it is fitting for the upright to praise him.
Praise the LORD with the harp;
make music to him on the ten-stringed lyre.
Sing to him a new song;
play skillfully, and shout for joy.
—PSALM 33:1–3

Doris married my brother over twenty-five years ago. Not only has she been my sister and close friend all those years, she's been my piano player since my college days. (No more math for right now because you'll figure out more than you need to know). Back when we had the Mike Courtney Trio — that's my brother — Doris was the piano player. And truth be known, it should have been called the Doris Courtney Trio. She has the real talent in the family.

Doris is petite. She weighs nothing and slips around as quietly as a butterfly. Her fingers move like hummingbird wings over the keys, and always on the right notes. And did I tell you she has perfect pitch? Play any note on any instrument and she can tell you what it is. Even hum a note and she can tell you what it is. Me? Spell out the note and I still have to think about it. But Doris is also a little clumsy.

I'm not trying to be ugly. But not long ago, Doris was going out with Sandi Patty and me on a three-day weekend run. Since we met at my house at midnight, we were anxious to get things loaded on the bus so we could crawl into our bunks and sleep. There were eight bunks on this bus and since there were only three of us, we had plenty of room for all our stuff. A junk bunk is what we call the bunk that catches all the clutter. I grabbed my favorite spot: bottom bunk toward the front, left side. For some reason, little Doris said she'd take the top bunk across from me. We'd barely made it out of my neighborhood when she hoisted herself up and then landed loudly on the floor between the bunks. We weren't even up to the speed limit yet! Little, quiet Doris said, "I think I broke my foot."

She suspected this right away because a few years earlier she fell down the stairs at my house and broke her foot for the first time. So she knows exactly what a broken foot feels like. And as luck would have it, she hurt the same foot this time.

We took the next exit to the hospital and spent three hours in the emergency room. Yep, it was broken all right. And pretty much in the same place as the last time. They wrapped her in a soft cast and sent her off.

"Do you want us to take you home?" I asked her.

She shook her head.

"Good thing you don't use your toes to play the piano," I said. When it comes to jokes to tell in a hospital, I got a million of them.

Doris trooped along with us, but a fresh break is painful and needs to be elevated. So we sang our songs with tracks and made do while she logged some hotel hours and room service.

To this day, little Doris is the only one I know of who's ever broken a bone on my bus, or on my stairs at home. Often times we'll have guests come along — wives, children, friends. But because of what happened that night, we've added a new bus rule. It comes right after "You must wear deodorant every day" and just before

"Potty in the hotel whenever possible." The new rule says "No children or Doris allowed on top bunks."

I can't be positive, but I believe when Doris fell, she yelled out in the key of B-flat. Even I could hear that one.

Chapter 7

Le Pari! Le Lost!

*E*ver been on a trip and got lost along the way? We, my whole family, got lost in France once—the country. Of course we didn't have a map. But we were only going to be there for four hours, "So why would we need a map?" David had said. I'm not blaming him at all, just wondering.

The deal was we were on our way to Senegal, Africa, to the city of Dakar, which is the westernmost point of Africa. We were going as guests of World Vision, an organization I've worked with for years. They wanted our family to meet with some of the families we were helping halfway around the world. But to get there, we had to go through France.

We had flown all night and had a four-hour layover at the Charles de Gaulle International Airport, so all we really wanted to do was get something to eat, wash up a bit, and wait for our next plane. Since we had no francs for food, David took twenty dollars and set out to exchange it. Not far from where we'd set up "camp" was a currency-exchange booth. David pulled a bill from his wallet and waved it before the man at the counter. I could hear David asking in broken English, "You change? To France money?" The man at the exchange booth didn't seem to understand David's broken-English, French-accented speech patterns until he said, "French fry money?"

"Ahhh! French fries!" the money exchanger spoke up, and he proceeded to swap our dollars for francs. Then he pointed to a McDonald's across the courseway.

Once we'd eaten and washed our faces, we still had a couple of hours to kill.

"You know," Chera, our daughter, said, as she studied a brochure she'd found, "the train runs right through the airport. We could at least go down and see the Eiffel Tower. I hate to be in Paris and not see that."

David said, "I guess we could ride a loop through town. See the tower and get right back, right?"

"Do you know how to get there?" Zach asked.

From the mouths of babes . . .

"It's a train that runs on a track," David said, like that explained everything. "All you have to do is find one that says it's going to the Eiffel Tower. Hop on, hop off, look at the tower, then come back." Chera had taken three years of high school French, so he asked her, "What's Eiffel Tower in French?"

"Eiffel Tower."

David shrugged and made some sort of motion to Zach, as if to say, how hard can this be?

So we took the stairs down to the train station and hopped on one that said Eiffel Tower. Since it was more of a subway than a train, we couldn't see anything along the way. We rode for about twenty minutes, then raced for the stairs up. It was cold and wet on the streets of Paris, and at first glance, I would have sworn we were in the Paris section at the EPCOT Center. The place looked that real! Quaint buildings, cafés, shops. We stood next to an ancient building —a cathedral is what it was—and gawked at our first glimpse of a

European city. We crossed a bridge that spanned a large, fast-moving river so we could get closer to the cathedral for pictures.

"I think that's Notre Dame," Zach said. He'd seen *The Hunchback of Notre Dame* a dozen times.

"I believe it is," I said, and laughed at how bright our son was.

"I don't see the Eiffel Tower," Chera said, making a full turn on the sidewalk, with no luck.

"We must not have stayed on the train long enough," David said, checking his watch, and tapping it the way you do when you're extra sensitive to time passing. "Oh well. Let's get some pictures of Noter Dame" — that's how he pronounced it — "and catch the train back." So we grouped up and had our picture made right there where Quasimodo lived.

"I wonder what river this is?" David asked. I could tell he wished he'd brought his fly rod. He'd fish in a bathtub if he had enough room for a back cast.

No one had a guess about the river. We didn't know of any cartoons of French rivers. And not knowing what this river was while we stood right above it just about drove David crazy. So he did the smart and sensible thing, I thought: he asked.

He approached a large man sporting a grizzled beard who was leaning against the bridge railing while he smoked a cigarette. "Excuse me, sir. But are you from here?" David asked politely (as well as slowly and loudly and with a French accent).

"Oui," the man said.

David glanced back at the children and me and smiled, like it was the funniest thing yet to be talking to a real Frenchman.

"Can you tell me the name of this river?" He pointed to the water, which should have made his question crystal clear.

The Frenchman took a long drag from his cigarette, and the expression on his face said it was a bitter drag. Then he pursed his lips and exhaled slowly so that the smoke circled above his head before being blown away by the trade winds sweeping up from Africa. "Le Pari," he said, pointing to the city around us with both hands, palms turned up. Then he pointed to the river in the same fashion and said, "Le Seine." Then he ended the conversation with a harrumph and poked the cigarette back between his lips.

David could have walked away. He could have brought that knowledge back to our group, back to our daughter who had three years of high school French under her belt, back to our son who'd seen *The Hunchback of Notre Dame* at least a dozen times, and we could have figured things out. But he had to clarify the geography with the Frenchman. "The Sane?" David said, in his best Southern American accent—very Southern even for someone from Tennessee, I might add. Maybe it was the jet lag.

The Frenchman drew down half the cigarette before blowing out more smoke and grumbled, "Oui, le Seine. Le Pari, le Seine." He did the open-palm pointing again—from the city to the river, back and forth, back and forth.

David nodded, and he seemed rather proud that he understood the Frenchman. "The Sane. Yeah, I've heard of that. Thank you very much."

When he walked back to us, he threw his hands up like it'd been all so obvious. "It's the Sane River," he said, and I saw the Frenchman throw his head back and let the trade winds blow up his nostrils. "I've heard of it lots of times," David said. "Wish I'd brought my pole now. Just to say I fished in the Sane River."

"Is it close to the Eiffel Tower?" Zach wanted to know.

David looked at his watch like he'd just remembered we had an appointment with a plane. "We'd better get back to the airport. Maybe we can see that on our way back home." So down into the subway we went. I don't think David is solely responsible for the long-standing strained relationship between France and the United States, but there's no doubt that diplomatic relations between the two countries took a beating that day, right there in front of "Noter" Dame and next to the "Sane" River.

We hopped back on the subway and this time followed our route on a map on the wall, noting each street as we passed. David noticed the fork in the track long before we got to it. "If we head that way," David said, tracing a finger along the map. "We're in big trouble." He chuckled like that would be a crazily impossible thing to happen. Five minutes later, we headed that way.

Not much exciting happened after that, so I'll spare you all the hurried French encounters that we had. Suffice it say we couldn't find a train to the airport. A Frenchwoman who spoke less English than we spoke French talked and talked and talked, but we figured she was telling us there was no way to get there from here. Finally, we began to communicate using an old game that the Pierce family is pretty good at: charades. We told her we wanted to drive (steering an imaginary steering wheel, changing gears, honking a horn) to the airport (arms outstretched to mimic the wings of an airplane; I believe this is "Get me to the airport" in any language). With a smile, she hurried us onto a shuttle that would take us to the airport, but we soon found out it was one that stopped at every hotel along the Seine River, with the exception of any close to the Eiffel Tower.

Have you ever been really, really lost? Now imagine that you can't speak the language or read the words, and you have somewhere to be soon, and the clock is ticking. Have I stirred up the stomach acids just talking about it? That's how I feel when I remember back to the time before I knew God all that well. Getting lost in Paris is nothing compared to that. It seems I zigzagged all over the place back then, with no real idea of where I was headed. The crazy thing is I was lost and didn't even know it. Since that time, I've been trying to learn the language (prayer), and I've been studying the map (the Bible) a lot more. And when in doubt, I just ask for directions. Here's how I navigate these days: if I'm over here and God is over there, all I want to know is, What's the shortest route from me to him?

That day in Paris we finally arrived at the proper gate for our plane headed to Africa with only ten minutes before takeoff. We were tired, beat, and wet (of course, it would rain on us — le Pari, le rain!) but grateful to be where we belonged. Grateful to be unlost. Just like being lost can cause my stomach to turn flips, being unlost brings an air of peace. Airport food never tasted so good!

On our way back to the United States, we had another long lay-over at the Charles de Gaulle International Airport. This time we exchanged a little more than twenty dollars for francs, then set up camp in McDonald's and supersized it for four hours.

Chapter 8

Wholly Ground!
Sweet, Solid Wholly Ground!

I've been around long enough, read enough books and seen enough movies, to know that when a day starts off just like any other day, watch out!

Well, this was one of those days. My road manager and I were in Nashville and had to head to Orlando. Just a simple, routine flight, right? At least it was until we heard *boom!*—no wait, it was more like *BOOM!* And then we smelled the smoke.

Our normal routine of a day began with us rushing to the airport—rushing because the traffic was horrible. Seems a cow had come off a truck and was illegally hogging the far left lane. Stuff like that happens in Tennessee all the time. Once we got to the airport, we checked our luggage, raced to the gate, and squirmed into the little seats on a very full plane. Some of my artist friends who live in Nashville were onboard too because we were all going to attend a World Vision anniversary celebration. Geron Davis was there. He's written some huge songs for the church. One of these is "Holy Ground." Yep, he's a friend of mine.

When the plane took off, I could tell something wasn't right. The thing seemed to struggle. I'm not sure how to describe that. But when you've taken thousands of flights and you know what a liftoff is supposed to feel like, then when you get a little bit of chug or a lurch (or some other short word with only the *u* vowel), you just know it's not right.

The pilot took to the PA right after the *BOOM!* Usually at this point he likes to welcome you aboard, tell you how much earlier than scheduled he was able to back away from the gate, point out that we'll be cruising at 37,000 feet rather than 35,000 feet because he's been out a couple of times already today and it's just one sweet ride a little higher up. And of course, he wants to tell you what the weather is where you're going, especially if you're going from a cold place to a warm place, and how much sooner than scheduled he'll have you at the next gate. But not this time. This time the voice seemed heavy laden, somber, full of gravity. The timbre of the captain's voice is another one of those things you just pick up after a few thousand flights. (Admittedly, this was the first time I'd heard the "somber" voice used.)

"Excuse me, ladies and gentlemen, but we are turning back to make an emergency landing." See how somber that was? "Please listen carefully to the flight attendants, and when we approach the runway, don't panic at the sight of the emergency vehicles following close behind us. This is routine for this situation."

Situation? This is not a good word. *Situation* can mean anything from an hour's wait for the next available table at Red Lobster to "We're looking for a bone-marrow donor now." Things got quiet. We held hands and prayed. Someone called out, "Geron, sing 'Holy Ground.' Sing 'Holy Ground.'" He didn't. My guess is he forgot the words.

We circled the airport a couple of times. We watched the emergency equipment shadow us down below—fire trucks, tanker trucks with big hoses, an ambulance. (Only *one* ambulance? How were we all supposed to fit in there?) My guess is they trailed us that way so that if we did go down, they would have as little travel time as possible before they could get to us and pull us out of the rubble and patch us up—after we fell one thousand feet at two hundred miles an hour! I made sure my tray table was up and in the locked position. That and a prayer, and we were ready for whatever happened. I hoped.

I began to think: have I done enough with my life, my gifts? I knew Geron had. He'd written "Holy Ground." He'd probably get into heaven on that alone. Would we nose-dive? Or would we grind along the ground creating sparks that would rush over the fuel tank, looking for a single spilt drop of fuel so it could do its blowup thing? Have I lived my life so that my kids will grow up to know God? Have my kids seen that the most important thing to me is Jesus, their daddy, and the two of them?

Angels must have set us down that day. I would have asked the emergency vehicle drivers when I got off if they'd seen anything at all flying around us, but they pulled away and disappeared as soon as we touched down. We applauded our somber-sounding captain. Geron began the chorus of "Holy Ground," and we joined in. A moment later, the captain returned to the PA, much more upbeat now, and explained that we'd lost an engine up there. But not to worry. We would be transferred to another aircraft, a more stable aircraft. He did tell us that these transfers usually take some time, but today a craft was close by and available, so we'd be heading out way ahead of our potential delay time. And that it was a steamy eighty-two degrees in Orlando.

Although at least a hundred lives were shook up, resolutions made, deals with God struck, tears cried, hands wrung, and prayers dispatched, I don't think our little in-air emergency even made the local news that night. I called my husband, and he surfed all the channels and said no, but there was a funny story about a cow on the interstate all morning.

Nothing like nearly crashing in an airplane to give you some perspective on life. Isn't it funny how we make deals with God? I wonder how many people on that plane that day actually followed through. Have you ever had a near-death experience? News flash: you're having one now! Even if you live to be a hundred, one day your life will be over. Our lives are short and uncertain. What will you leave behind? What do you hope to leave behind?

Not long after this gimpy-plane experience, I was heading to Dallas. I'd had a few days home, long enough to slobber all over my family and to tell them how much I love them, and to tell them how much I love God, and to make sure they had a typed copy of my funeral plans (and extra copies to be distributed to all the guest speakers) in case anything should happen to me.

Sometimes I worry about whether I'm doing the right thing. That's a big bump in the road for me: whether my kids are okay with my job and my being gone so much. After all, it is just a job. I could always quit. I could go into journalism and do news stories about cows falling off the backs of trucks.

When I got to Dallas, I checked my email, and here's the note my daughter sent me:

Mom,

I miss you too. Sometimes I do get really tired of your job (as I am sure you do), but I know that there are thousands of men and women out there who have been ministered to, and I wouldn't trade that for anything. You're doing the right thing—I believe that, and I am proud of you for it. Not only are you a great comedian, but a great mother. That's gotta be tough! I love you, Mom. Now go kick some Dallas butt!

Chera

And so with her blessing, I'll continue to keep kicking, one "situation" after another.

ROADKILL REPORT

The Road—
Don't Leave Home without It

A person's steps are directed by the LORD.
How then can anyone understand their own way?
It is a trap to dedicate something rashly
and only later to consider one's vows.
—PROVERBS 20:24–25

I was wrestling with the room service, trying to order breakfast after
normal breakfast hours, which happens a lot when you zigzag around
the country and you get off your bus and into a hotel late and all
you want to do is eat so you can stay alive—but I digress. One
reason I was having such a hard time with the room-service man was
because I was worried about David. The last time I'd seen him he
was standing in the middle of the street, in the pouring rain, waving
goodbye while water slowly filled the brand-new hole in our driveway
behind him. In a way, I was almost afraid to call him.

I'd been home for a few days and had gotten a chance to rest
up. And since it would be for only a few days, everyone thought it'd
be a good idea to just park the big trailer loaded with speakers and
lights and such, which we were pulling behind the bus, parked in
my driveway. "It'll save us on storage costs," one road-savvy person
said. So we did just that. George, my bus driver, backed the mini-
house into my driveway with no problem and unhitched it there.

Part 2: Bumps in the Road

Five days later, a new driver showed up and ... let's just say his skills weren't as sharp as George's. Actually, he backed up to the trailer just fine. David even stood behind him, a couple of minutes before midnight — the time most bus trips start — and guided him back like an air-traffic controller. With a crank of a handle, they clicked the trailer right into place.

The rain began to fall around the time the trailer got stuck — not stuck in mud like you might think since it was raining, but the trailer sunk so low that the hitch dragged on our drive, right at the end, and would go no farther. That's when the substitute bus driver had a really bright idea: he'd get a running start.

With a rev of his giant diesel engines (now it was a few minutes after midnight, and the neighbors' houses had been dark for some time), the bus lurched forward, tugging the heavy trailer behind it.

I don't think anyone stopped to think that if the hitch dragged the first ten times at a slow speed, what would make it not drag with a full head of speed? Answer: nothing. The bus hit the street and turned right. The trailer dug in and scraped and moaned and grated as the metal hitch quarried out a basin, which quickly began to fill with rainwater. I watched the whole thing from the back window of the bus.

As we pulled away, David just waved — or maybe he was shaking his fist. It was hard to tell in the dark, in the rain. I could see his silhouette, however. There was enough light coming from the neighbors' houses now to see that.

I planned to call him the next morning, just as soon as I could. I still wasn't sure what I would tell him, though: "Hey, honey. That's just life on the road?... in the road?... under the road?" Maybe I'd tell him, "Just think of this as another one of those road lessons we have to go through. Right, dear? Like 'digging in' when we don't feel

like it, or ... oh, I know: when the routines in life make us feel ...
well, stuck. Then we just have to put the hammer down and — gun
it!" Yeah, he'll buy that. That's a good lesson.

But first, I needed pancakes.

Part 3

Hi Chonda,

I have a concern about one of the garments we'll get when we go to heaven. I'm fine with the robe of righteousness and the garment of praise, but I heard a preacher talk about a gown of salvation, and that kinda scared me. My first image I got when I heard the word gown was of a hospital gown. You know, the ones that are open in the back? I really don't want to be caught running up and down the streets of glory with my flaps blowing in the breeze, and I'm pretty sure the saints behind me wouldn't be too thrilled with that either. What do you think? Should I pack some Velcro strips just in case?

Chon
123
Any

ROAD WEARY

It doesn't matter how you travel it,
it's the same road.
It doesn't get any easier
when you get bigger,
it gets harder.
And it will kill you if you let it.
—**JAMES BROWN**

Fatigue is the best pillow.
—**BEN FRANKLIN**

Chapter 9

A Red, White, and Blue Thank-You

My day started off with my son, Zachary, calling me in Mobile, Alabama, and telling me they'd caught Saddam Hussein. Zach was fourteen at the time and kept up with the news more than most adults do.

"They got him, Mom," he said. "They got him." Zach knew this was an important win for freedom. Despite all the talk about weapons of mass destruction and 9/11, he knew that this was one bad man who would no longer do anyone any more harm.

Zachary's been to a few places that have made him appreciate the freedoms we have here in America. In western Africa, we learned that many people there believe that if they suffer daily trying to find food and water, it must be God's will, and it's useless to try to change that. The result is that people continue to live in squalor, and children die.

And Zachary's been to Israel with us. He stood at the edge of the Jordan River where Moses had led his people out of four hundred years of slavery and bondage and said, "It's not a very big river." I think what Zach meant was that if all those people had to do to be free was to cross over this river, what took them so long? I mean, they knocked out the Red Sea in an afternoon. A whole sea! This was a river, and not a very big river at that.

In many ways, Israel reminded us of Tennessee, especially around the Sea of Galilee, which is surrounded by hills and trees and hotels and restaurants. Sometimes it seemed we were only down the road from home. That is, until we saw the schoolchildren.

They were getting off a ferry that had been to the other side of the Galilee. Most likely the twenty to twenty-five children, maybe seventh graders, had just returned from a field trip. They carried schoolbooks and backpacks and all wore the same blue and white uniforms. As the children ran down the ramp, they giggled and raced and shoved and crowded—just like kids will do at home. But what wasn't like at home was the image of the teacher, who followed in the rear with a rifle draped over his shoulder, right where a backpack filled with snacks should be.

He filed off the boat behind the children, laughing and calling out instructions just like any teacher would. A couple of times the gun shifted on his back, its barrel pointed to the ground, and he'd casually hitch a thumb in the strap and straighten everything—as casually as a chaperone back home will adjust his fanny pack.

We discovered that this is not only the way of life for Israeli children; it's the law. A few years ago, Israeli schoolchildren were frequently targeted by terrorist groups. So now whenever at least ten children are gathered for a school function, the teacher must carry a rifle. He just checks one out at the front desk like we'd check out a Ping-Pong paddle at a rec hall. The students seemed to think nothing of it. (I can still remember how ominous my history teacher Mr. Darrow appeared because he wielded a wooden paddle with little holes drilled in the flat part to decrease wind resistance and thus increase paddle speed—so the legend went.)

"That's a little scary," Zach said, trying not to make any sudden movements until the school group passed by.

Shortly after that, we discovered a McDonald's in Jerusalem — one of the few places in Israel where you can get a real cheeseburger, and so we did. At a nearby table sat a group of young people, most of whom were soldiers. In Israel, everyone must serve in the military once he or she graduates high school: three years if you're a man, two if you're a woman. And one of the requirements is that you never go anywhere without your rifle. On duty or off, that baby's with you!

And so this group of young people, who were sitting close by, eating fries and talking and laughing, probably about boys or girls, just like they do back home in Tennessee, all had rifles. And not just any rifles, but Uzzis — fast, convenient, and deadly. (Don't worry. I'm not going to make a McDonald's joke here.)

But despite that, there in McDonald's with supersize fries and a chocolate shake, I was almost feeling at home. That is, until one of the young people/soldiers stood up to put away his tray and knocked his rifle off the table he'd laid it on earlier so he could eat his burger.

Me, David, and the kids about tossed our fries. But the soldier casually reached down and picked up his weapon, never missing a beat with the story he was telling. We finished our food and took the shakes with us.

So Zachary has gained a real sense of freedom, which is so often taken for granted in places like back home in Tennessee. He's also very aware of moments when men as evil as Saddam Hussein are taken out of the world equation. When Zachary called to tell me that, I wanted to give him a big hug, to feel him alive and safe in my arms. And I would do that just as soon as my plane landed back in Nashville. Of course, I couldn't tell him that because I was afraid he'd run and hide. He wasn't quite secure enough in his freedom for open hugs yet, or so I thought.

My flight was delayed in Mobile, but I didn't get too bent out of shape. Happens all the time. When I got to Atlanta, someone with the airline asked if I'd like to upgrade to first class—because I fly so much. That happens a lot too, and I always say yes, even though it is only a fifty-five-minute flight from Atlanta to Nashville. First class has the best pillows.

In first class, I was surrounded by military. And I could tell from their conversations that they were just returning from Iraq.

I said to the three soldiers nearest me, "My son tells me we got him today."

"Yes, ma'am."

"Yes, ma'am."

"Yes, ma'am."

"I want you to know I appreciate what you guys are doing over there."

"Thank you, ma'am."

"Thank you, ma'am."

"Thank you, ma'am."

I was rapidly feeling old and motherly. "Nice weather we're having."

"Yes, ma'am."

"Yes, ma'am."

"Yes, ma'am."

Just then a fellow soldier walked by and those oh-so-polite soldiers razzed him good about enjoying his coach seat.

Oh no, no, no, I thought. Not on my shift. I stood and demanded that he take my seat, but he would have none of that. So I grabbed up all my things (and my first-class pillow) and all but ordered him to take it. I'd have it no other way. It was my motherly prerogative. As I made my way back to coach, I heard him say, "Thank you, ma'am."

Before the plane took off, I called the kids to tell them about the nicest bunch of soldiers onboard, all coming back from Iraq. "We should do something for them when they get off the plane," I said.

"Like what?" Chera wanted to know.

"I don't know," I told her. "But something with ribbons — red, white, and blue ribbons. Think of something and meet us there. You can't miss them; they're wearing camouflage."

Since the kids had only an hour to scramble, I didn't expect too much. I just wanted to thank these soldiers somehow.

I was one of the last passengers to get off (because I was in the back of the plane now), so I passed little knots of families hugging and squealing. And sometimes a soldier would grab someone up in a bear hug — a wife, a child, a mother — and would twirl her around in circles, and whoever was getting spun about would be crying and laughing and snotting all over both of them, so I had to watch out for that.

Then the foot traffic slowed and seemed to bottleneck just past security. As I got closer, I could see why: there were Chera and Zachary and my husband, David. They had a couple dozen Coca-Colas with red, white, and blue ribbons tied onto the necks of each, all long and loopy and patriotic. They passed them out to each soldier that walked by and said a simple, "Thank you." I don't think I'd ever been more proud.

I caught up with my family and helped pass out the rest of the colas, and I could tell the soldiers were very appreciative:

"Thank you, ma'am."

"Thank you, ma'am."

"Thank you, ma'am."

When all the gifts were gone, I turned to do what I'd been dying to do ever since I'd heard Saddam Hussein had been captured: hug my son. I caught him in a momma hug and pulled him close. I was expecting a little resistance but not what happened next: Zachary picked me up! He squeezed me right back and then lifted me off the ground. My feet probably cleared the floor about two inches. Zach is taller than me but as round as an ink pen. He may have lifted me, but there was not going to be a twirl—not this day. But maybe that was the very same thing all those others who'd been twirled throughout the airport that day had said once.

The power of a thank-you can make you do something like that—hug someone and spin them around. There may not be a more freeing experience in all the world than twirling in the airport with someone you love.

What other ways can you think of to say thank-you? A phone call? A card? A smile? My experience is if you can break open with gratitude, you can move mountains—or at least lift a road-weary soldier.

So I wanted to say thank-you to the soldier I'd given my first-class seat to and to the two dozen soldiers we'd given colas. I wanted to say thank you for your hard work, for your sacrifice, for making us all free to hug and twirl whenever we dare, without the requirement of lugging a rifle with us everywhere we go.

I wanted to say thank-you, but there weren't enough first-class seats or colas in the world. But if there were and I could, I know what they'd say—each one of them. Something like, "You're welcome, ma'am."

Chapter 10

The Night
I Took Up Farming

*T*he night started off with no one knowing who I was.

A security guard with a big belly met us at the back entrance of the fairgrounds somewhere up in the Northeast, and Shannon, my road manager at the time, told him who I was and what I was there for.

"Sorry," he said. "I don't know nuttin' about it. You'll have to go to the front gate."

The front gate was just across the field, a couple dozen fence posts down. I could see the thing from where we were blockaded at the back gate. But we backed up anyway and crept over to the front gate. "Hello," I said. "I'm Chonda Pierce, and I'm here for the concert tonight."

"Yes," the woman with red hair said. "Tonight is the Chonda Pierce concert." Only she pronounced my name with a hard *ch* sound and not the soft *sh* sound like it should be.

"She *is* Chonda Pierce!" Shannon nearly screamed.

Finally, after much haggling, we got through and parked our car where the others were parking, and someone who looked like he was in charge met us there in the field. In the ten minutes it took us to walk from there to a big barn only a few yards away, he called me Sandra, Shonna, and even Samone.

The barn was one of those big dairy barns, the kind that can hold herds of cattle. Even had I not read the sign on the way in, I would have known this is a land of much cattle by the fresh cow patties that were covered with a thin layer of fresh sawdust. There was a time in my life when I used to want to run away to the circus (doesn't every little girl?), but tiptoeing through this smelly minefield confirmed that I'd made the right decision. In the circus, they have elephants, you know.

The man in charge left us in the barn so we could do a sound check. This was the first time I'd ever tried to get the highs and lows right with a demolition derby going on next door. We tested between crashes, and even then it was hard to tell if the sound was my voice or a car bumper falling off.

As we were finishing up, the man in charge asked if we were hungry. Truth was we were starving! The smell of popcorn and caramel apples and grilled onions had my stomach doing flips. So the big man reached into his pants pocket and pulled out a few bills and handed them to us. "Well, we don't fix no tables or nothin'. But here's some money to go get you somethin'."

I took the money and made a beeline for the funnel cakes. Shannon got the corn dogs, and we shared. While we nibbled, we moseyed over to the arts-and-crafts display and marveled at what you can do with macaroni and lima beans. In the 4-H shed, a couple of calves eyed my leather pants more than I was comfortable with. Had either one of them said anything that even slightly resembled the word *Momma*, I'd have been on the bus and out of there. We watched people throw tennis balls, softballs, and even bowling balls at targets made of milk jugs and dinner dishes and furry cats. I nearly won a rabbit by dropping a Ping-Pong ball into a fishbowl filled with colored water.

We watched a runaway horse smash into a parked minivan. Some kid with a grating voice, amplified on a loudspeaker, kept barking out how much fun it was to shoot a water gun into a clown's mouth and win a prize, when suddenly he barked, "Hey, aren't you Chonda Pierce?" I grinned and waved at him and figured that's what it would feel like to run away with the carnival and have everyone there know who I was.

Every now and then I'd get a good whiff of sawdust, and that would send me right back to youth camp in South Carolina and everything was just fine. I watched them put a blue ribbon on Margaret's hand-stitched quilt and another one on Ethel's canned peaches before turning back to the barn.

The activity backstage was a good distraction for me. My opening act was as fun to watch as a tractor pull. He dressed in hot clothes and sweat almost as much as he complained. He complained about having no air conditioning, other artists, other managers, about how much he sweat, and other ventriloquists. Yes, he was a ventriloquist. After a big dose of his complaining, I tiptoed away (my tiptoeing skills had been greatly sharpened since that afternoon) and told him he might need to be alone so he could practice keeping his mouth shut. I don't think he got it.

When I finally got onstage, I had some real zingers for them — fresh from the county fair. I told them that this is where my pants were born. And I thanked the 4-H department for their love and care of leather. From where I stood, I could see the fried dill-pickle cart and Sammy's Smoked Sausages. I wondered where they had been while I was eating funnel cake. I wondered how much of that spending money we had left. I made a mental note to send Shannon out during the first break. When I broke into a song there at the end like I usually do, I nearly started a stampede in the lower forty, until the soundman was able to pull down some of those high notes.

I don't do too many county fairs. A dairy barn is a hard room for comedy (so is a cornfield, a racetrack, and the stage area next to the Himalaya). But I will probably do more county fairs if I have the opportunity, and it's not just because of the funnel cakes either.

Sometimes I think I can see God at work in his people. I see them raise their hands to honor and worship God. I may see a tear. I may see someone kneeling to pray or someone mouthing every word to "Blessed Assurance." And as wonderful as all this is to see, I realize what I see may still only be as thin as a fresh layer of sawdust. What I have come to learn lately is that from my vantage point on that stage, I cannot know how *deeply* God is working. I may never know what sort of seeds may have been planted by a song I sang or a story I told. But that night God gave me just a glimpse.

After the concert, I met a young girl, and we talked for a moment. Finally, she threw her arms about my neck — sticky from the cotton candy — and said, "Thank you for coming to our fair. Nobody important ever talked to me before." I was touched. But I also wanted to kick the ventriloquist and his dummy. He had twice the opportunity I had! But the greatest moment came later that night when the wife of the fair-board president told me, "I can't get my husband to darken the door of a church, but he really loves you. And I was so excited that he was willing to have a Christian entertainer at the fair this year." Now there's a seed in the ground that you don't have to be a 4-H member to recognize.

Sometimes we have to get our hands dirty. Farming's just like that, you know. I remember going to my Papaw's house when I was a little girl. I wouldn't see much of Papaw during the day because he was always out planting seeds. He'd come in at dark, dirty, bent over, and weary looking. And just when I thought he should collapse on the sofa and start snoring, he'd smile and say something like, "Gonna have a good crop this year."

That night I was not just Chonda the comedian, or even Shonna or Shondra or Simone. I wasn't even plain old Chonda (with a soft *sh*). I was a proud farmer, planting seeds for a future harvest. Weary or not, it's all about the planting, folks. And for that, the president's wife might as well have pinned me with a blue ribbon.

ROADKILL REPORT

The Chonda Cam

Never tire of doing what is good.
— 2 THESSALONIANS 3:13

I wish I could strap one of those cameras to the top of my head for a day, just so you could get a firsthand look at what it is I have to go through sometimes — a Chonda Cam! I would edit this heavily, of course, especially the boring parts, like the five hours I had to spend in the Houston airport the other night. You would not enjoy watching that at all. Just how many times did I look up at the Departing Flight Information board? About three hundred? Yes, I would trim that down to a handful, and then for only a second or two each time — just so you'd get the idea.

I was right in the middle of a Christmas tour with 4Him. We called it "Four Guys and a Fruitcake." (At least I got a title role.) And you know how the weather can be in Texas around Christmastime: wet! I was in Houston and had to get to Amarillo for the concert, but I was thinking about skipping Amarillo and renting a car and driving on to Dallas to meet the bus as it came through the next night. Suppose I had the Chonda Cam on just then. Of course, to watch five hours of me driving through a soaking rain might be boring TV as well, so I'd have to cut most of that too — unless something exciting happened, like a jackknifed trailer rig filled with explosives, teetering on a high precipice, or a bridge out up ahead with people cloaked in soggy parkas standing in the road and waving their arms for all to either stop or plunge to their certain deaths. For that, I would be glad that the Chonda Cam was rolling tape.

Fortunately, that night I didn't have to rent a car. My manager called and said he'd found something even better: a private jet, and it was waiting just for me. Now *that's* exciting stuff, and I would make sure that the Chonda Cam recorded every second of something like that. I was about to be whisked away like Elton John to a show that just "had to go on."

Maybe "whisked" is a bit of a stretch. It was more like a slow shuttle. And the shuttle sort of whined across the tarmac like a lonely cat. But that was okay too. If the Chonda Cam were rolling, we could speed up the tape and play loud music. At least I was getting the VIP treatment.

Now, I'm no math whiz, but I was good enough to figure out way ahead of time that my "whisking away" time was eating up all my preparation time. Not to panic. I went into my do-what-you-got-to-do mode. If I were taping this part, I'd ask someone to dub in the theme song from *Mission Impossible*.

I raced into the ladies' room there in the hangar and washed my hair in the sink, only to find no towels. No problem (theme music still playing). Since I still had my luggage with me, I dug around to find my cleanest dirty shirt and dried off with that. Then I rubbed on some fresh makeup and climbed onto my private jet, where two kindergarten children smiled at me from the cockpit. "Good evening, ma'am," one of the children said in a voice that had apparently made it through puberty. (This would really blow your mind on the Chonda Cam.)

We made it out of Houston and landed in an Amarillo parking lot, or so it seemed. A car was waiting for me, running and warmed up just like they do for the big stars. I jumped in and found dinner prepared for me: a Diet Pepsi and a Kit Kat bar. I would probably have to get permission before showing these items on the Chonda Cam because of all the strict legal licensing laws. And if I couldn't get permission, I would have to get one of those blue dots to cover the names Diet Pepsi and Kit Kat because they are registered trademarks.

I made it to the venue and raced into the back of the church just as intermission started, which was great because I really felt the need to brush my teeth. I would not show too much of me spitting into the sink on the Chonda Cam because that would be poor taste and not exactly quality TV. After that, I raced out and took the microphone, and I'm sure most people probably thought I'd been backstage all night, napping or playing solitaire on my laptop. But the Chonda Cam would easily prove them wrong.

And if I did have Chonda Cam on my head that night, and you had been there in the audience in Amarillo, you would be able to see yourself on TV (once the tape was made). I would try to pan over the audience slowly so that when you spotted yourself, you could pause the tape and wave to yourself on TV for as long as you wanted. I'm sure in the editing I would put fun music over the moving pictures and make the special-effects guys lay in sparkling things that look like fireworks. And I would speed up some parts and slow-motion other parts so that in the end my little trip in a private jet from Houston to Amarillo would look like the most exciting thing you'd ever seen.

So in the end, if I wanted to give you a glimpse of what it's really like out there on the road sometimes, I guess the Chonda Cam wouldn't work after all — unless you watched the entire eight hours of deleted scenes, which would include the whole two hours of me staring at the Departing Flight Information board in the Houston International Airport, with no music whatsoever.

Chapter 11

If I Had a Dumbwaiter ...

*F*unny how people, places, dates, and events can weave themselves into a fabric that we call "story." Not long ago, I was in Richmond, Virginia, a place steeped in history. About seventy miles away in Charlottesville, you'll find Monticello—the home of Thomas Jefferson. And that's where I was headed in a rental car, to find my husband and son. You see, our tour bus came rolling into town just as another bus did; only this one was filled with about a hundred sixth graders, and one of them was my son, Zachary. And one of the chaperones onboard was my husband, David. It was David's birthday, so I set out to find them in the hills of Virginia. And this is the first thread of this story.

I called a car-rental place, and they brought me a sedan and a map. When I told them I was looking for Monticello, a young man began to tell me a story about the house and how young Thomas Jefferson did this and that and something about the Louisiana Purchase. "Do you know that Thomas Jefferson invented the dumbwaiter?" he said. "Yep, you can move stuff from upstairs to the basement—in a snap!" He snapped his fingers to show me just how quick a snap is. He had more stories to tell, but I had to take off because there was a little restaurant right near Monticello where the sixth graders were having lunch.

When I found the place, I couldn't believe I'd found the place. The building was old and tucked into the woods and decorated to look like it'd been there for two hundred years. Even the waitresses and waiters dressed like the pictures of people in my high school history book. Inside the restaurant, kids were swarming everywhere. I found David standing in line with a leg of something on his plate (chicken? a small cow?). He had that glazed-over chaperone look in his eyes, so he never saw me coming. I spun him around and gave him a big birthday kiss right in front of the children. After all, Virginia is for lovers.

I think he and Zach were glad to see me. David grabbed a tray for me, and Zach carried it. We sat at our own table, away from the other chaperones and sixth graders and talked and giggled like we hadn't seen each other in ages. It'd only been about four days, but there's something strangely wonderful about meeting someone you love and haven't seen in a long time in the middle of someplace you've never been before. After lunch, we held hands as I walked David and Zachary back to their bus. I told David about the last few nights of the tour, and he told me this fascinating story about the world's first dumbwaiter. "I never knew that," I told him.

I cried all the way back to Richmond, partly because I already missed David and Zachary (they were on their way to the White House) and partly because I was lost. I had no idea where I was supposed to go. After about five phone calls and three U-turns, I made it to the hotel.

"How's Monticello?" the car-rental picker-upper asked.

I was a bit embarrassed and was sure he could tell I'd been crying, so I said, "The dumbwaiter broke." I left him with his jaw hanging to the ground. He could have used a dumbwaiter just for that.

The theater we were in that night had been built in 1928, during the peak of the vaudeville days. It was ornate, gorgeous, huge, gaudy, and full of statues—naked ones. We were trying to decide what to do about them. Cover them up? Should we? That sounded like something my grandmother would do. I wondered if she had ever been in this theater because we were in the town where she'd been born. And that is the second thread of this story.

I doubted my grandmother had ever been in this particular theater because she was born in 1899 and would have been twenty-nine at the time this theater was built and well on her way to raising a fine Christian family, which would be my Aunt Ruth and Uncle Gerald and Mom. But it was highly possible that my great-grandmother hung out at the theater, might have done business there. My great-grandmother had lived in this area too and probably had more stories to tell than Jefferson or Washington put together. Her house probably had a name too, one well known by the local police. You see, not long before this trip, I found out some interesting things about my family tree, and the roots of it were sunk deep right here in Richmond, Virginia.

No one knows the whole story of my great-grandmother. Those who did were never asked, and of course, no one ever wrote any of it down. She came into this world, lived her life, then passed on, and all we know about her this far down the line is that she had five children, and all five were separated at a very early age and spread across the country. It seems great-grandmother's job—although proven to be the best way to *produce* children—was not the best way to *raise* them. (Okay, that's as close as I'm getting. Are you with me so far?)

Anyway, my grandmother and all her brothers and sisters grew up and raised families and never knew where the others were until one day almost forty years later. I'm not sure how it all happened.

Someone found someone, and they found someone else, until one day my grandmother got a call from someone who said, "Hi, we're you're long-lost brother and sisters, and we want to get together." They picked the airport in Louisville because it was a central place for them to fly into. My grandmother had never been to an airport before. I read about this reunion in a newspaper article someone in the family had cut out long ago. The article had pictures too, and even in the old black-and-white grainy shots, I could see happy smiles. I couldn't see all five people clearly in the photograph because they were all trying to hug at once, and it looked more like a big gray-and-black mass with arms. An octopus maybe. But it was evident that there was something joyous about meeting up with people they hadn't seen in a long time, in a place none of them had ever been before.

But back to my grandmother. She came into this world with a ton of garbage on her shoulders. I heard she was raised by a couple in Kentucky who longed for the days of slavery, just so they could have one. But because slavery had been illegal for nearly fifty years, my grandmother was as close as they could get. She worked hard and did her best, and one day she ran away from home and married my grandfather. Not long after they were married, she was invited to a tent revival by a neighbor. That's where she found Christ, introduced him to her new husband, and that's where together they sloughed off the weight of the past—hers and others. That's also when and where that branch of my family tree got lopped off, only to be grafted into the glorious family tree of God.

But the past often heals over in an ugly scar, always there to remind us. Right? I dug up the details of this old story because I was standing there in that old theater that day, wondering. I felt heavy, maybe a bit oppressed by the history—*my* history. And even though it's a history already covered by grace, Satan will still use it as a tool, a weapon against me. I've been beaten with it many times. Sometimes

I've even handed it to Satan, handle first, and all but asked him to take a good whack.

We worried a bit before the show about the naked statues. But only a little bit. After all, they were only marble or granite or whatever it was they used for naked statues back then. Actually, I think someone later told me they were made of plaster that'd been poured into a mold. So somewhere in this world is probably a whole factory that makes nothing but naked statues. Is that still considered art? And somewhere in this world there is probably a company that makes nothing but molds for making naked statues. (Okay, how many times have I said "naked" already?)

I don't think Satan gives a hoot about those statues. But our memory, our past? Now there's a stronghold. And *there's* reason to fall on your knees and pray for strength and, at the same time, pray for God to tie, bind, and rebuke the deceiver. For that's the power we have in our new family. So before the concert that night we prayed for cover—not for the statues, but for *us*. For protection. For peace. We claimed victory, and we made sure that we remembered just what family we really belonged to. And that's a story with a happy ending.

From Monticello to a vaudeville theater; from Thomas Jefferson to my great-grandmother of questionable character; from a rendezvous in a quaint, woodsy restaurant to a grand reunion of brothers and sisters in an airport; from a dumbwaiter to naked statues. It's funny how the threads of all these stories weave themselves into a pattern that I have no control over. I know this because if it'd been up to me, I'd have woven them all into a few big blankets and covered all those naked statues. And then I'd have checked around to see if the old theater had a dumbwaiter and, if it had, would have sent every one of those statues straight to the basement—in a snap!

Chapter 12

A Bad Case
of Unfunny

Some days I just don't feel very funny. And that can be a real problem since I am a comedian. Coffee helps, and chocolate's even
better, but neither lasts for very long.

The funny thing about being funny is that when I don't feel so
funny, I can fall back on what I know. Most of the stories I tell I've
told a thousand times before. I could tell them in my sleep! So I'll tell
these stories and people will laugh, and I'm always surprised because
people are laughing at my jokes even though I don't feel very funny.

So what sort of things would make one not feel funny? How about
a week after the 9/11 attacks? Volunteers from all over the country
had traveled to New York and were still searching for survivors, and
over 350 firefighters and policemen were still unaccounted for as I
began a "Four-Eyed Blonde" concert in Huntsville, Alabama. For
those of you who don't know, Huntsville is Rocket Town. This is
where Wernher von Braun went to work after he finished developing
the A-bomb during World War II.

President Bush was giving a major speech that night about what
our country was going to do about the Taliban, while I was telling
jokes about growing up a preacher's kid in the South. My manager

huddled in front of a little TV backstage and filled me in on the details during intermission. He told me we were now officially at war. Okay, deep breath, I thought. Now let me go out and do the second half of the show. Oh yeah, I've saved some real zingers for the second half.

What I really wanted to do right then was to stop the show and say something like, "Look, rocket people of Huntsville. We're at war now. Surely you have something, a top-secret weapon thing of the likes that the world has never seen. And if that's the case, then maybe now would be a good time to call the president. We're at war, people!"

But instead I told them stories about broken baptisteries, Wal-Mart shoppers, and a Chevette I once owned. I didn't feel a bit funny that night, but we laughed anyway.

You know another funny thing about being funny? The times when you feel like laughing the least are usually the times you need to laugh the most.

Another time I absolutely had to be funny was one day a couple of years later when we shot the *Have I Got a Story for You* video. We'd rented the beautiful Elco Theatre in Elkhart, Indiana, and sold out two shows for the day. The plan was to tape both concerts and use the best footage, which meant I had to wear the same outfit. So for most of the first show, I was so worried about sweating too much that I sweat twice as much as normal. Thank goodness for those camera angles shot from high up.

I had a crew the size of a small city working on stage design, lighting, sound, cameras. We'd even hired a couple of guys whose job it was to drag around electrical cords all day so people wouldn't get tangled up and fall. We were paying union wages, and everyone working that day was at least an eight-hour drive from home. So there was no way we were going to cancel the shows.

The main reason I didn't feel funny that day was because just before I'd flown up to Indiana, my mother (nearly seventy then) had fallen and broken her back. I'd left the hospital and gone straight to the airport to make it to Indiana on time. When I left my mother at the hospital, she was flat on her back—except for the three giant pillows I'd stuffed under her for support—and begging the nurses for another shot of that last thing they'd given her to ease the pain, please?

Twenty-four hours later, I was on a stage that was magnificently lit with at least four cameras rolling tape and was trying to be funny. And since I was telling all new jokes, I really had to concentrate. The last thing I wanted to do was to give away the punch line and then have to back up and say, "Oh, that's not it. I think it was one English-man and two Frenchmen. Or was that one Hungarian?"

I get asked a lot, "What do you do when you don't feel funny?" All I can tell them is that I just go out and do it. If I waited until I felt funny, some days I might not even get out of bed. When I don't feel funny, I just be funny. Pardon my grammar. But if I can just do that, then most likely that funny feeling will come loping in sometime before the night is over—late, yes, but at least it shows up.

And you know what else? Sometimes I don't feel very spiritual either. I mean, who does feel like they're sitting in heaven's great room 24-7? We're human. We feel tired, we feel beat up, we feel lonely, left, betrayed, empty, and weary. On those kinds of days, feeling spiritual seems like an ancient memory. During those times, if someone tells me I should feel spiritual, I want to make him see heavenly stars.

So what do I do when the spiritual meter points to the low end? Same thing as with the funny: I just do. I listen to praise music, I sing praise music, I read my Joyce Myers and Beth Moore books, I read my Bibles (NIV, NASB, Living, King James, and the Message). If I depend on emotion, emotion will let me down. So I do what I know. And the funny thing about feeling spiritual is that if you just do what you know, just be spiritual, eventually that feeling will return, will come loping in.

Feeling funny is nice. Feeling spiritual is nice. But don't confuse emotion with the real thing. Emotions ebb and flow. The truth is solid.

Let me tell you what happened to our family just a few Christmases ago. We inherited a nativity set. That sounds like a strange thing to inherit, but my brother was moving out of town, and he had one of those nearly life-size sets—the entire set: Mary, Joseph, Jesus in the manger, all three wise men, two camels, and a sheep. They were big and plastic and painted in bright colors and each one burned a single 40-watt bulb. That's 360 watts when fully lit. We built a stable from scraps of wood and brought in a bale of straw, and the whole grouping was quite nice. Very Christmasy.

Then a few days before Christmas, I had one of those days when the Christmas spirit just left me. I wasn't feeling it. In fact, I was a scrooge—snapping and barking. Maybe you've been there? I shouldn't have been surprised at how I felt because it was the same old Christmas craziness: everyone seemed rushed, everything seemed so expensive, traffic was too slow, *It's a Wonderful Life* had shown eighteen times already and so far I'd missed every single showing. I guess the last straw was when we came home from the mall late one night. It was wet and cold and windy and—did I mention that all the players of our nativity scene were hollow plastic and quite lightweight? It doesn't take much of a breeze to tip one over and just a bit more to send them off sailing.

We pulled up in time to watch part of the tumbling show. David called out their names as they passed through the car's headlights: "Mary! Joseph! Jesus!" In a blink, our lovely family had been scattered all over the neighborhood. Wise men were upended in the ditches. A camel grazed in a holly bush. And the worst thing of all was having to knock on the neighbor's door late at night and ask for

Jesus back. And after I'd pressed the neighbor so hard at Easter too. He just rolled his eyes and said, "Make up your mind, will you?"

Yeah, that pretty much killed the Christmas spirit for me. So what did we do? We regrouped, literally. First, we rescued all the nativity players and placed at least one good brick in the base of each figure. We discovered that the tumble had pretty much knocked out all the bulbs, but the good news was that David had some spare bulbs in the garage.

Now that the figures were better anchored and more than fully lit, David plugged in the nativity set and—whoa!—heaven came down and rested in our front yard! And just like that, the Christmas spirit was back.

I love my job as a comedian. And I'm convinced that what's kept me going as long as I have (fifteen-plus years now) is understanding that big gaps can, and so often do, open up between emotion and reality—funny versus not funny, spiritual versus nonspiritual, Christmasy versus non-Christmasy. When that happens, I stay busy. I do what I do, and I do what I know until that gap has a chance to close up. And when it does, hold on. Because for me, that's when a smattering of laughter becomes rollicking guffaws, a quiet reverence becomes *Hallelujah!* And plastic nativity characters light up the neighborhood with at least 900 watts of brilliant white. Seems we were out of 40-watt bulbs, so David used 100s—nine of them. Now that's the spirit!

ROADKILL REPORT

The Big Hose-Down

I have swept away your offenses like a cloud,
your sins like the morning mist.
—ISAIAH 44:22

When I finish an evening concert, I like to get back on the bus, talk
about the night with the crew, maybe eat some cottage cheese and
hot wings, and then get some sleep. Once I go into sleep mode,
nothing had better wake me. Know what I mean?

I'd been after our bus driver the last few days to give the little
bathroom on the bus a touch-up whenever he got the chance, but
the days went by and things were starting to get a bit gross. Part of
the bus driver's duties is to keep everything on the bus vacuumed,
polished, and deodorized. This particular night, our bathroom failed
the sniff test miserably (which consists of me opening the door
and taking a big whiff). Plus we were out of toilet paper. With
twelve people on the bus, that just wouldn't do. I told John before
I crawled into my bunk just how important cleanliness is to me. He
smiled like he understood.

Late into the night, as we were cruising down the interstate, I
heard the rain falling against the bus. This was not so unusual, but
the rain was pounding so hard that I thought real cats and dogs
were falling down on us. I'd never heard rain like this before. From
what I could tell in my windowless bunk, it was coming down in

sheets out there. I could actually hear the layers of water passing from the front of the bus to the rear. Then I figured I must still be a bit groggy because I thought I heard the roar of the rain move from the rear of the bus back to the front — then from the top to the bottom, and the bottom to the top! I'd heard of sideways rain before but never zigzag rain. I put my hand against the wall there in my bunk and felt that the rain was sure enough passing over in strange waves. Maybe this was something like crop circles, only with rain. Other than that, the ride was as smooth as glass.

So I did what I always do when something on the bus wakes me: I crawled out of my bunk and staggered sleepily to the front. It didn't take long to see that we weren't moving anywhere. And John wasn't behind the wheel. I pulled back the curtains on the window, and there he was outside — with a long, high-pressure hose in his hands, blasting off the road dust from the side of the bus. Matt, my road manager, came shuffling out from the back of the bus as well. He took a look out the window and said, "Is John washing the bus?"

I couldn't say anything. Instead, I stood and walked to the back to let Matt do his job, which is partly to handle problems and discomforts we may incur while traveling to our next venue. While I was an inside clean freak, seems John was an outside clean freak. I was afraid this wasn't going to work. "Kill him," I called over my shoulder and crawled back into my bunk and dreamed about rain.

I awoke to see that Matt had disobeyed a direct order and that John was still alive. But how could I stay angry at John for too long? He'd only been trying to clean up. Perhaps he had this thing about bugs splattered on chrome. That's not exactly something you talk about over hot wings and cottage cheese, but I could appreciate that.

Part 3: Road Weary

I stumbled to the bathroom, rubbing the sleep out of my eyes, and was instantly hit with the spring aroma of fresh lilacs. One quick look, one quick sniff, and I instantly forgave John for the late-night wash and rinse.

Wouldn't it be nice if forgiveness could be bought with something as simple as a Glade air freshener and a new roll of toilet paper?

Part 4

Dear Chonda,

 Do you still have that Chevette you talk about on the Four-Eyed Blonde video? If so, two words for you:

yard art.

Chor
123
An

A BEND IN THE ROAD

It's a dangerous business,
Frodo, going out your door.
You step onto the road,
and if you don't keep your feet,
there's no knowing where
you might be swept off to.
—BILBO BAGGINS, *LORD OF THE RINGS*

When you come to a fork
in the road, take it.
—YOGI BERRA

ce
Lane

JSA

Chapter 13

A Slow To-Go Box to China

*M*ost Thanksgivings I stay at home. Even workhorses like myself know when they should be home with their families. So I made a grocery list that included more turkey dressing than I would ever need, pulled out my Christmas dishes (because Christmas starts at Thanksgiving at my house), and prepared for family. And wouldn't you know it? The one day I decide to dig in and surround myself with family, the other side of the world knocks on my door and sits at my table—I'm talking about China. This was new territory for me. A definite bend in the road.

My daughter, Chera, had called ahead from Auburn University and asked if she could bring her physics-lab instructor home for turkey. "She's from out of town and has nowhere to go for Thanksgiving," she said. "And that just doesn't seem right." I agreed, then I scratched through the "one pound of dressing mix" on my grocery list and penciled in "one and a half." Later Chera called back and said, "Oh, and she has a friend."

"Who has no family?"

"Yes."

"Bring her," I said. Then I made that "two pounds of dressing mix."

Ten minutes later, Chera called once more: "And that friend has a friend who has no family."

"I'll get three pounds."

"What?"

"Just bring them."

"One other thing, Mom. This is their first Thanksgiving in America. They're all from China."

I penciled in soy sauce and noodles on my list—just in case. I didn't know.

"They don't speak much English," Chera added.

I was already starting to regret this.

"And I don't think they believe in God," she said.

I clamped my pencil with my teeth and began to roll up my sleeves. "Bring 'em on," I said.

"Red and yellow, black and white, they are precious in his sight!" I love that song. And I was looking forward to being on the mission field with Chera, even if it was only in our living room. And that's what I worried about most—our living room! Or them being in the room with the rest of my family, anyway. I was worried that our friends from China might get the wrong impression of America by visiting *our* house—by being in the same room with my brother and husband. In a situation like this, Mike and David are too unpredictable.

Our guests from the other side of the world that weekend were two beautiful young women, Cha and Bin Ying, and a most pleasant young man, Chow Kan. (And there's no way I've spelled any of these names right.) They arrived at our house with smiles and overnight bags stuffed fuller than a Thanksgiving Day turkey. And Chera was right: they spoke very little English. We welcomed them with smiles and handshakes and bowing (bowing seemed the right thing to do). They gathered with the rest of my family there in the great room, where the football game was on TV. It was hard to tell if they were fans of the game or if they just liked it because of the bright colors and the uniforms (like I did). So I left them alone.

What David and Mike did later — as soon as I turned my back — convinced me that the two of them would never represent our country well on the mission field, or at the UN. So it's good that neither one of them gets out much. I overheard my brother telling our guests about the Pilgrims and about that first cold winter with little food. He said they'd been so thankful to the natives for the extra food that they all did what is traditionally known as the turkey dance — a dance we try to emulate before dinner each year (which doesn't look much different from David's 1970s disco days). They're sick, I know! Thankfully, the turkey dance didn't catch on.

Zach was probably the one most fascinated with our guests. He moved with giddiness from a vase to a picture frame to a tea cup and lifted each one and turned each in circles until he found what he wanted to read to our guests: "Made in China." Then he'd grin and say, "Thanks, Chow Kan!"

When the family gets together for a holiday like this, we like to find a table game and play it as if the outcome were a matter of life and death. We figured this was a good, American tradition to share with our travelers from so far away. First we tried Pictionary, but when Chow Kan drew his card, he had no idea what a marshmallow was, or a moose, or a pet rock. So we put that game away. Then Zachary yelled out, "We could play Chinese Checkers!" They laughed. One of the girls said, "Our English not that bad!" But their English was not good enough to play Catch Phrase, Outburst, Word-Up, and definitely not Scrabble. Finally, we settled on a game that cut across all cultural and socioeconomic boundaries: Monopoly. Or as Chow Kan called it: Mono-Polo.

Later, while Chow Kan built hotels on Park Place and Board-walk, Cha and Bin Ying helped me peel potatoes, then giggled when I mashed them into a pudding. If that was weird, then I figured I'd better warn them about the meat. My brother, Mike, likes to hunt and bring to the table his wild game for the family — a duck, a deer, or a quail. Of course, I didn't know the Chinese word for a single wild animal. And when I tried to explain these animals to the girls, using as much body language as possible to show feathers and antlers and turkey struts, I realized I was pretty close to doing the traditional turkey dance that the Pilgrims performed so many winters ago. Our guests just grinned and nodded at me as if they totally understood the importance of this ritual to our society. I made a note: no dessert for David and Mike.

Our guests' English seemed to improve as the day went on. Or maybe they were more comfortable with us (a turkey dance can do that). Cha talked about her country and their family traditions. They have "Autumn Day," she explained, a time when families gather. But Chinese families are small, she said. They are *allowed* to have only one or two children. We talked about what happens if someone has more than that. And the stories were such sad ones to be told at a time of thanksgiving.

I watched Zach's face as Chow Kan talked about the restrictions of his childhood and what he called the "regulation of government" in Chinese life. I asked them about God, and my mom asked them about church. They had heard of church in China. Bin Ying and Cha had even slipped into one just to hear someone speak English. Cha said, "Some go to teach the English to do the mission work." She asked me, "You have job?" I told her, "I do comedy to do the mission work!" She could not understand how comedy and mission work go together. "Don't worry," I said, "neither do many folks over here." That was my best line all day!

We surprised Chow Kan with a birthday cake. He turned twenty-three that Thanksgiving. Tears welled up in his eyes when he said, "Thank you so much. My first birthday in America and my first birthday cake. I will never forget." After our Thanksgiving meal, David and Chera took our out-of-town guests on a three-day hiking trip in the Smoky Mountains. They'd never seen snow before. It was fun watching them get packed. They did not bring many hiking clothes, so David and Chera stuffed their bags with extras, which got used up real quick once they hit the ice. And they saw plenty of snow and ice on this trip. Walked on it, slept on it, fell in it, made snowballs with it and threw them. (This is another thing that seems to cut across all cultural boundaries. Even if you've never seen snow before, you know what to do with a snowball!) "I'm from south China," Chow Kan said late at night in his windblown tent. "I've never been this cold in my life." That Thanksgiving he was thankful for the extra clothes David and Chera had packed.

But before the hiking trip, before our Thanksgiving meal, we stood in our traditional family circle and prayed a prayer of thankfulness to a God who makes all things possible. I couldn't help but grin because I knew, in all the movement and the confusion and the language gaps and the made-up dances, what had really happened here that day. There were my nephews Josh and Jacob, both tall and talented and men of God. My brother and his wife stood next to them; their lives are what miracles and *Oprah* shows are made of. Mother and Dad made us all laugh again, even though they don't try. (They don't speak a word of Chinese either, but they were able to slow their speech down and talk louder for the sake of our guests.) My cousin Brad was there with his beautiful wife, Vicki. Brad is now a music minister in Cynthiana, Kentucky, but we go way back, over twenty years at least, to when we were just two kids playing country music in a bar. Each of us is a reminder to the other that God never gives up on anyone. My son, Zachary, stood taller than his dad. My once tiny preemie is strong, funny, and brilliant. Chera Kay stood only a few feet away, in the middle of her "mission field" — Cha and Bin Ying on one side and Chow Kan on the other. I doubted she had a clue of what she'd done. She'd planted a seed that week and had allowed us to water it — with games and talk and food and laughter. Generations could be affected, generations all the way on the other side of the world! I'd never been to China before, but it looked as if our love, at least, was going to make the trip. We can always do that, right?

I squeezed my husband's hand, the man who is the love of my life, who leads this household, and on a day like this, I was so honored to simply be his wife. Oh yes! I had so much to be thankful for. Almost made me want to do the turkey dance.

Chapter 14

What's behind Me Gets Smaller Every Day, Hopefully

*T*he bus pulled into Greenville, South Carolina, early one morning, where the people talk normal and the azaleas bloom in the spring and the moon is always full—*always*. If you've ever been to the Greenville-Spartanburg area and seen the giant water tower painted to look like a peach, you know what I mean. (You've heard of *Left Behind*? Well, in Greenville-Spartanburg, they have the "whole behind" at the top of a hundred-foot tower.) I pointed this oddity out to Sandi Patty, who I was on tour with at the time, in front of a packed house, and then told her, "Don't worry, it has a leaf or two!" Had she been taking a drink of water just then—possibly from the peachy water tower even—she might have drowned.

For some of you who know me already, you know I can't talk for very long before I tell you how much South Carolina means to me. I grew up there, in towns like Orangeburg, Rock Hill, and Myrtle Beach—a place where a kid could make a good living finding shark teeth along the beach and then selling them to a place called the Gay Dolphin. (I believe they've since changed the name to the Happy Dolphin, for obvious reasons.) My sisters and I went to youth camp in South Carolina, I kissed my first boy in South Carolina, I broke my arm in South Carolina, and my childhood family began to break apart in South Carolina.

When I go to South Carolina for a concert, I can fill the room with old friends and cousins—and I do. A lot of people there knew my sisters, Charlotta and Cheralyn, and they'll meet me after the shows to tell me how much I look like my sisters, and how they would be so proud of me. Many times people have met me after concerts to give me pictures of myself and my family, and each grainy photograph will be loaded with memories—most of them good, all of them powerful, sometimes too powerful to get my mind around it in a single moment. That's what happens to me when I go to South Carolina. I always fancy that somehow a little bit of South Carolina air will always be settled in my lungs. So how, then, can I believe that a place so familiar could be a "bend in the road"? Sometimes the familiar can be a hard place to go back to.

For Sandi, South Carolina is a reminder of a time in her life that is still tender with pain. She talked openly that night about a time when everything was wrong and falling apart. She wanted forgiveness, from that audience. You see, her "story" broke nationwide from Greenville, South Carolina. She's an Indiana girl, and at that moment all those years ago, crushed under the load of her already convicted heart, all she wanted to do was get back to her children and to her family. Can you imagine every step you've made—good and bad—being printed in every magazine and tabloid? What if your worst sins were written out for the world to see? Your children to read? Your mother? Hanging like a giant peach in the sky? I don't think I'd ever leave my house again, much less subject myself to the discipline and guidance of my pastor and my church as Sandi eventually did.

For Sandi, South Carolina was a long way from home, in more ways than just the miles.

Don't take this personally, South Carolina, but that night our hearts raced with years and years of emotions, shared by our whole crew, from incidents that took place ten, twelve, fifteen, even twenty years before. But a familiar sight like sand, azaleas, or an old street; or a smell like salty air, newspapers, or furniture polish in a little church can cause old memories to come rushing to the surface from the deepest of depths.

What I discovered in Greenville that night is that God is more powerful than even the toughest memories. When you plow through, when you're determined to follow Christ, you'll discover God's presence. And *that* is a powerful thing.

Here's how we plowed through that night. When the show was over, we stood on the stage—me, Sandi, and anyone else who would say "It's time to move on!" The crowd was gone. We took a small box of baby wipes (good for the strongest of jobs, if you know what I mean), and we each washed our hands while tears rolled down our faces. We bundled up our little vanilla-scented wipes that reeked of years (but only to us) and left them there on the edge of that empty stage. That's how we built a vanilla-scented altar. No rocks or bricks. Just the tears from our faces and the stains of past hurts, which looked like nothing more than regular grime from our hands. This time we walked away from those hurts, leaving behind a lot more than baby wipes. We had to leave because, no doubt, there'd be another bend in the road ahead, and probably not too far away either.

I've written about the weight of the past on the present before. Sometimes you may dwell on the past; it may loom so large that you can't seem to help but live with it every day. That's the kind of thing you have to knock loose with a stick and then cover it over deep with God's grace. Bury it. Then sometimes you round a familiar bend and—*wham!*—you get hit with something you totally forgot about.

For that, a prayer and some baby wipes ought to do the trick. It worked for us that night. When we rolled out of town a little later, it was too dark to see the giant peach, but we knew it was there, knew that it hung over us, and behind us, like a new moon.

ROADKILL REPORT

Mopeds in Mexico

For he will command his angels
concerning you
to guard you in all your ways.
—PSALM 91:11

I guess the nearest I ever came to being real roadkill myself was that time I took a moped trip across the island of Cozumel in Mexico.

Yeah, yeah. I know some of you are saying, "Cozumel? Wow, how lucky." But some of you who've driven a moped are probably nodding your heads and saying, "Oh great. Just as I was about to put the pain of my moped story behind me, she goes and stirs up memories of my painful moped story."

I got invited to work on a cruise ship for a week in January not long ago. Bring the whole family, they said. So my husband and Chera and Zachary were pumped up to be heading to the tropics for a few days in the middle of winter. On one of these days, we ported in Cozumel. The cruise organizer told all the artists that we had a choice that day for recreation: we could either shop around in more shops like we'd already seen hundreds of, or we could all come along for about a twenty-mile round-trip ride across the island and back, making our way along the beautiful shoreline and through tropical forests on mopeds. "It'll be a once-in-a-lifetime opportunity," he said. I voted for more shops, but I got outvoted by the kids—and David.

Part 4: A Bend in the Road

In the end, we had ninety people fitted out on mopeds. I don't
think you can look much sillier than when wearing one of those
moped helmets. The guys from 4Him, Mark Schultz, Avalon, they
all put on those helmets, which have a way of making your head
look too big — except on Rebecca St. James. She still looked cute. I
should have known it was a bad idea when some out-of-control kid
in the parking lot revved his bike and the thing shot out and crashed
into a parked van, right in front of David and Zachary. (No, it wasn't
Mark Shultz. That's what I first thought too.) David and Zach's
helmets knocked together, and they laughed about that, which made
me feel safer already.

We headed out in groups of thirty. The plan was to make it to a
remote café on the other side of the island, have an exotic lunch,
then motor back, enjoying the scenery along the way. Good plan.

In Cozumel, there are no special driving lanes for mopeds. We
were lucky there was even a road. I did not realize this until a couple
of miles into the trip when we zigzagged along narrow, tree-lined
roads and one car after another whizzed by in the other direction.

We made it to the café alive but sunburned. Two others were not
so lucky. I saw twisted ankles and scratches and bruises and, yes,
even blood. "That moped seemed to have a mind of its own!" one
witness said. "We could get killed out here!" said someone else. "Are
you going to eat all your fries?" another one asked me (one of the
4Him guys, I think).

We rode back with the echoes of these fresh horrors in our
minds and hugged the right shoulder more than necessary, with our
helmets strapped on tighter than necessary and our skin smothered
with SPF-30 sunscreen.

Halfway back to the ship, on one particularly sharp curve, I
feared I had just witnessed suicide by moped. An older woman who
could have been my mom took the curve in front of us without

slowing the least and without even trying to turn. Or so it seemed. She shot through the curve and completely disappeared, deep into the rain forest. Just disappeared. *Poof!*

David braked hard, and he and Zach hopped off the bike they shared and ran to the edge of the road. They spotted something, and in a moment they disappeared into the forest as well. I began to feel queasy. I feared we'd be showing up on one of those reality-TV shows, something like *When Vacations Go Bad*. A few seconds later, up came the driver, scrambling through the brambles on all fours, with scratches on her arms and twigs poking out from her helmet in camouflage fashion. Otherwise she seemed okay. I got close enough to the edge of the embankment to see David and Zachary lugging her moped up the steep incline. "That was so cool," I think I heard Zach say.

We still had a few miles to go, and now we were shaking. "Let's keep it slow," I suggested. And we did a good job of that until we got off the winding road and back on the main highway. I could see the moped shop not too far ahead. I must have gotten anxious, and when I'm anxious, I tend to be a bit reckless. I did what Zach later called "gunned it." My moped zipped forward, and the little bit of hair that poked out from beneath the sides of my helmet swept back like wings. My eyes watered so much that I was barely able to see the big city bus that was coming on me fast. I couldn't steer away, nor could I slow down. I thought about the woman who had *poofed!* into the rain forest earlier. But a rain forest is a much softer place to land compared to the front end of a bus. So this is how it ends, I thought. Like a bug on a windshield!

I prayed and I squeezed the handles. Now where did that brake go? I squinted. I may have even yelled. I'm not sure. What I do know is that somehow, at the last possible second, I pulled the bike and leaned to the right and veered off to the right shoulder just in time.

Air from the bus wooshed by. I thought I heard a bug smack against its grill. No silly helmet or sunscreen could have protected me from that.

When I pulled into the rental lot, someone had to help peel my fingers from the grips. David, Zach, and Chera made it in shortly after me, and I told them my story. I was supposed to perform that night on the ship. How could I be funny after this near-death experience on a Mexican highway?

I think it was David who said the most healing words that day, words that helped me move past this horrific experience and slowly erase that image of the oncoming bus from my mind: "So you want to go shopping or something?"

Let this be a cautionary tale for you. Learn from my own nightmarish experience. If you're ever in Mexico and it comes to a choice between drinking the water or riding a moped — I can't think of why a situation like this might ever occur, but just in case — then drink the water. Besides, those helmets really are the silliest-looking things you've ever seen.

Chapter 15

A Fitz
at the Ritz

*T*he Ritz-Carlton on Amelia Island, just off the coast of Jackson-
ville, Florida, is where the rich go to pretend—for the briefest
of times—that they are the superrich. I went there not long ago and
would go back in a heartbeat, if for no other reason than for the free
superrich samples they leave out for you in the bathroom. Of course,
they had little bottles of shampoo and lotions and shower gels like
most hotels will give to you. I recognized those. But there was also
a bar of glycerin soap wrapped in gold paper (I saw the same ones
later in the gift shop for three dollars!); a couple of shower caps; little
emery boards to touch up my nails, all neatly packaged in cardboard
slips with *The Ritz* printed on the outside; a tube of shoe polish and
some buffing cloths; and tiny boxes of little cotton balls, which I
wasn't sure what to do with. And the luxury didn't stop there.

Hanging in the closet were his-and-hers matching bathrobes.
And at night while we were out, someone would leave a yellow rose
on my pillow. (I gave David the benefit of the doubt, but he admitted
that he didn't know where "that crazy thing had come from.") Even
the toilet paper was monogrammed. And had my initials been RC,
I'd have been tempted to take that too. The sad thing was we were

surrounded by all that wealth (ostentatious, we poor folks who work crossword puzzles might say), and no sweet tea was to be found anywhere. That's why you'll usually find me checking into the Holiday Inn, where the coffeepot, phone, and ironing board are all right there in the bathroom with you — talk about multitasking! And sweet tea is only a phone call away, just the way I like it.

For that one night, I did my comedy thing and people laughed. Only sometimes it was hard to tell if they were laughing with me or at me. My sweet-tea joke bombed, and so did my "A rich man died and went to heaven" joke. It was a tough room, but in the end, they gave me a standing ovation. Go figure. What I secretly hoped for was that at the end of the night, a grandmotherly woman would approach me, with tears in her eyes, and say something like, "Oh, Chonda. You're so funny and talented and the 'rich man died and went to heaven' joke just slayed me. You are the granddaughter I've always wanted but never had. The doctors tell me I have only six weeks to live (and that was a month ago), and I want you to have everything when I'm gone."

And I would say something like, "Well, thank you, Mrs. Carlton. I do hope you enjoy your last two weeks at the Ritz-Chonda."

David and I went back to the room, slipped into our matching bathrobes, and ate chocolate until we were sick and he passed out on top of a yellow rose. The next morning is when David woke up with yellow petals pressed into his cheek and said, "Now where did that crazy thing come from?"

"It's a rose, dear. People give them to the ones they love."

"Well, they shouldn't put them on a man's pillow. That's just wrong."

We left early that morning. And, no surprise, a stretch limousine met us at the front lobby to take us to the airport. I was about to enter when someone called out my name. Only he called out, "Mrs. Pierce!

Mrs. Pierce!" I looked around for David's mother. A short man with glasses and black curly hair approached me and told me that even though he was a Jewish man, he found my speech to be very entertaining as well as very spiritual. "Do you mind if I give you a word I have from the Lord?" he asked.

Oh boy. This is usually when I run. Too many times people will blame the craziest things on God. I braced myself. But my conscience was clean; I knew I had a suitcase full of just the stuff you're allowed to take, like soaps and gels—not bathrobes or towels or pillows or the TV remote control. "Sure, go ahead," I said.

The man straightened himself and took a deep breath before he spoke, as if he'd been running: "First comes peace. Then joy. Then love. And finally understanding." He took another deep breath and waited while I soaked that in. I pondered what he said, and still do to this day. The order is curious. I always thought understanding might come before peace. But the more I thought about it, the more this man made sense. First, stop the unrest, the uneasiness; find peace. From that place, where breathing will be easier, the joy will flow. Now with peace and joy, love may follow. Then only when we are close enough to love will we understand, will we even care to understand. These words sounded to me like necessary links in a chain that could possibly connect us all together. Take out one link and you have division. And with division, you have a different sort of chain—one that is laden with violence. These words coming from a Jewish man who had possibly seen his share of violence made sense to me.

My limo was waiting. I thanked the man for his insights, for being a vessel for God, and ducked to enter the door.

"Oh, one other thing," he said. I straightened. He smiled and seemed to be debating whether to tell me this other thing or not. Finally he said, "Your name. It's funny, but would you like to know what it means in Yiddish?"

"Yes. That would be nice." Wow, this would be like stopping at one of those kiosks in the mall where they have an ancient-looking chart handy and, for a price, you can find out all about your ancestry and what your coat of arms looks like. I wanted to know about my Jewish-derived name. (Of course, when Mom named me, she was only trying to think of something pleasant-sounding with a soft *sh* sound that was spelled with a hard *ch*. She knew nothing of Yiddish.)

"In Yiddish," my friend said, "the word is *aschounda*. It means 'a shame.'"

Wow. I didn't see that little bend in the road coming. I must have had a blank look on my face, because he tried to explain (with a smile): "You see a kid walking to school and he drops his books and you say, 'Oh, that's *aschounda*.'"

I don't think my expression ever changed from the earlier blank one. I was pretty speechless. Frozen in disbelief.

"Oh well," he said. "I enjoyed your performance last night. Have a nice trip back." And my new friend left.

David held the car door open for me. Then he pointed to one of his ears, made a motion like he was poking something into one of them. "Guess that's what the cotton balls are for, huh?" Wished I'd gotten those too.

David was right. And one of my prayers is that he doesn't read this far into the book, or he will be impossible to live with. But people will say things, sometimes purposely to tear you down, sometimes unknowingly. And even though it may sting at first, or even for a long time afterward, we can't let what someone says get inside our heads or under our skin, where there are too many soft organs to damage. We may not have a choice the first time we hear those stinging words, but we certainly don't have to hear them again—usually spoken in our own inner voice because we can't let it go. Put some cotton in your ears. (I'm speaking metaphorically here.) And if you don't have any metaphorical cotton, then do what David does: stick your fingers in your ears and go "nah-nah-nah-nah-nah-nah-nah-nah" over and over again.

All in all, it was a pretty ritzy weekend—roses, chocolates, and glycerin soap—and I might have come away with an overall pleasant experience despite the absence of sweet tea, if it hadn't been for that last-minute family-heritage insight. And in the words of my new Yiddish-speaking friend, "That's *aschounda*."

But in the words of my longtime husband: "Nah-nah-nah-nah-nah-nah-nah-nah-nah …"

Chapter 16

Laughing in the Dark

*O*ne day, and not so long ago, when everything seemed to be running smoothly, when career and life and family seemed to be clicking along just fine, I broke. What I thought to be "clicking along" turned out instead to be that long, slow ride to the top of the steepest roller-coaster hill. If you've ever ridden one of those big rides, you know the sound I'm talking about. You can probably also guess what happens next.

In Miami, Florida, I reached the top of that hill, and then the bottom fell out and I began one long, crazy ride that made me fear the whole car could leave the track at any moment. The best thing about the next three weeks is that I lost about fifteen pounds. And the worst about the next twelve months? Well, I'll probably write a book about that later, but for now I'll give you a brief glimpse of what it's like to laugh in the dark. So hang on. The ride gets a bit bumpy through the loop-the-loop.

I happened to be in Miami with my best friend, Alison, my manager, Nicole, and my business manager, Michelle, because we were there to treat a new friend and hard worker from North Carolina to a girls' weekend out, with all the exfoliation and mud packs you can pack into a weekend. Our new friend was the winner of a contest we'd held for our Turbo Hosts (what we call a superhelper for the concerts) who'd helped us make the "Be Afraid" tour so successful.

We were guests in a swanky hotel that pampered us like queens with room service and little chocolates on our pillows at night. We were smack in the middle of massages and manicures and pedicures and scented saunas. This was supposed to be a time for us to take a nice, deep breath and enjoy our little reward to ourselves in south Florida while winter raged back home. Just relax and breathe a little was all we had to do. When suddenly I couldn't breathe at all.

Something seemed to snatch my breath away, like the worst of one of those giant roller-coaster rides, only I was in a swank hotel room and we were trying to decide what fancy place we'd be having dinner at that night. If I could have chosen a time to fall ill and be whisked away to the emergency room, it would not have been then and there. (Especially since the place we'd decided on for dinner has the best desserts!)

Since the breathing problem wasn't so bad that I needed anything like a tracheotomy, I went to the emergency room in a cab. Patiently I lined up with the rest of the injured and ill and waited for my turn. This also gave me time to make phone calls and line up all my insurance information — plenty of time.

Four hours later, when it was my turn to receive emergency care, the doctor began by examining my lungs. He listened to me breathe through his stethoscope. He thumped and prodded and asked me kindly each time, "Does that hurt? Does that hurt?" He X-rayed me from the front, then from the back. My blood pressure was extremely low by then, enough of a concern that the doctor started an IV drip and wanted to keep me overnight for observation. We missed dinner, Alison and I, but at least our nails looked great.

Alison had been with me all afternoon and all evening when my husband finally showed up to relieve her. This was the weekend David and his buddy Ken, Alison's husband, had gone to the Dominican Republic for some scuba diving. He was on his way back and happened to be changing planes in Miami when I called him.

By the time he rode over in a cab and walked into my little cubbyhole there in the ER, I'd already been stuck and prodded all over, to a point where sometimes I'd say, "Yeah, as a matter of fact, that does hurt." I had tubes in my arms, wires hooked to my chest, and I was woozy from the stuff they'd given me, which they said would help me to relax.

"Hey, hon," he said, threading his arms through the tubes and wires to give me a hug. "I thought you were supposed to be having fun this weekend."

I smiled, or at least that's what I think I did — meant to, anyway. "Do you like my nails?" I said, lifting a hand for him to inspect.

Not much medically happened after that, not in Miami anyway. They did take me down to X-ray a few more times to shoot more pictures from different angles. They drew blood, lots of blood, and continued with the IV drips. Alison went back to the hotel, and David stayed with me. "I'll just hang here in this chair," he said, and he did. Neither of us slept much that night, and it wasn't because of uncomfortable chairs or the fact that I was sick. In case you've never been there, the Miami emergency room in the wee hours of the morning is like a war zone. The woman behind the curtain next to us was a grandmotherly Jewish woman from New York. She had no family there with her, and the family she did have back home in New York was worthless (so we overheard), and she wanted more pain medicine than they were giving her. And if she didn't get the pain medicine soon, someone was going to be in real trouble. These are the sorts of things she moaned (sometimes screamed out) all night.

Two curtains down, a gunshot victim was rolled in on a gurney, then was wheeled away shortly after that, and a lot of people were crying. The woman from New York swore at those who cried close by but would not give her more pain medicine. This was also Super Bowl Sunday, and David would wander in and out from the lobby. I remember him telling me that Janet Jackson had done something wacky, but it didn't make sense, and I blamed it on the drugs — mine. Then sometime in the night, long after the football game, with David still in the chair beside me and the woman from New York continuing her appeal for more drugs, a man pushing a floor-buffing machine made a few passes around my bed. David mumbled and stirred enough to raise his feet to give the guy room. Now my nails and my floor were both well polished.

Since this was to be the last day of our trip, all my girlfriends had planes to catch. It was 6 a.m. when David finally stopped one of the nurses and asked when we would see a doctor. She stopped, rolled her eyes to the ceiling, and blew out a puff of air. "Maybe in two hours when he comes in," she said.

"We want to go home now," he said.

"The doctor will have to sign you out."

"So how do people get out if they want to just get out? I mean, you can't just keep us here, can you?" He looked back at me. "You tell me she needs rest, but there's no way she can rest here. This place is a zoo — but the floors look nice." Here he smiled. "We need to go home. She's not getting any better here. Plus, that will give you more time to work on her." David hitched a thumb toward the curtain that separated us from the woman who promised blood vengeance on all the doctors and their families if she didn't get more pain medicine right away.

The nurse puffed again. "You'll have to sign an AMA." Against Medical Advice.

"No problem."

We were out of there in twenty minutes and went back to the hotel to clean up and then off to the airport to catch a plane home. I was better but weak.

Over the next few days, just as I'd begin to feel better, I'd quickly take another dip. Now I was afraid that the doctors in Florida had missed something. At home, they checked me for parasites, since I'd been in Mexico a couple of weeks before. The way they check you for that is they give you a strong medicine that will kill any parasites. So you take the medicine and watch and see if you get better. "This will kill anything," the doctor said, shaking the bottle of horse pills in one hand while making notes on my chart with the other. "And I want to give you a steroid," he said. "This will help build up your system."

"Will I be able to lift cars?" I was joking.

He studied my charts. For a moment his face darkened. "Do we have your insurance info on file?"

"How about pianos?"

"Excuse me?"

"Yes," I said. "Good insurance."

Then he lightened up. "No, you won't be able to lift cars or pianos."

During the next two weeks, I went to the emergency room about six times — every time because I couldn't breathe, or couldn't get off the bathroom floor without help (now I could see the importance of the constant buffing and waxing of tile flooring). David would load me up and pull up to the drop-off zone. He was rather calm and coolheaded about each trip, except for when he'd walk me (sometimes wheel me) to the nurses' station. Then he'd act a bit flustered and panicked, and that panicked energy seemed contagious and got me wheeled to my bed faster. They let me keep my wristband, and we got to know all the nurses by name (some of them had even seen my videos). Other than the being ill part, we had a lovely time.

Each trip to the doctor's office usually meant a different medicine. Now, I'm a firm believer in medicines. Get sick, take medicines. But by now my coffee table looked like a showcase for the next Doctors of Medicine Convention (if there is such a thing).

Word of my near death made it back to my pastor (okay, so I called him), and he and his wife came over and prayed with me. When he saw my collection of drugs, he called in Dr. Westmoreland, our friendly neighborhood surgeon. The doctor introduced himself and then proceeded to prod about my gallbladder area. "If it's your gallbladder, I can cut that out," he said.

"Take anything you need, Doc," I said. "Just make me better."

"First of all," he said, "let's pray." And he knelt beside me and prayed for healing and wisdom from the Healer on high. After that, Dr. Westmoreland pointed to the coffee-table pharmacy and said, "And let's get rid of some of these." He picked one up and read the label. "Steroids? Take enough of these and you can lift a car." He smiled. "Not really." I didn't think so.

So I cleaned off my coffee table, and the next day I drove to town for a gallbladder test (drink this, X-ray that). According to Dr. Westmoreland, everything looked good, and he seemed very disappointed. He'd already sharpened his knives.

He didn't get his chance to cut me, but he did send me to his doctor friend, Dr. Knox. Seems that Dr. Knox has his own video crew and camera, and both are rather small. He put me to sleep, and when I woke up, I had a brand-new video. I guess I could call it *Chonda: An Inside Look* or *What Happened to All the Krispy Kremes?* But fortunately, because of doctor-patient privileges, it'll never be shown.

The problem it seemed, according to Dr. Knox, was not in my lungs but rather in my stomach. So the doctor asked me, "Have you been under an unusual amount of stress lately?"

I thought for a moment. "No. I don't think so."

"And what do you do for a living?"

"I'm a comedian."

His face darkened. "With insurance?"

"Very good insurance."

He smiled. "The life of a comedian sounds wonderful. Laughter is good for you. Like a medicine. Travel much?"

I made some quick mathematical calculations and answered, "About one hundred fifty dates a year."

His eyebrows lifted, but I wasn't finished.

"And I just finished my fifth video—not counting the little piece we just did through the tonsils. I'm working on a book too. I'm nearly finished with an eighty-city tour and—"

"Stop!"

"What?"

"You've got to stop, or at least slow down."

He wrote me a prescription for a couple of more things: acid reflux, depression, anxiety. But that one piece of advice to slow down would prove to be the hardest pill of all to swallow.

Slowly, I began to move again, but slowly was what I wanted. My manager cleared my calendar. And for the first time in my career, I had to cancel concerts. This broke my heart, but it's just what the doctor had ordered. Slowly, I began to move about my house again, to even go outside of my house again. After a few weeks, I even slowly went back to work. Just a little at a time though.

At the time of this writing, I'm still learning the art of going slow. It's hard work and needs to be constantly refined. And even though I'm allowing God to teach me patience, I feel I am a poor student. Sometimes I try too hard and want to learn patience as quickly as I can. All my life I've gone at breakneck speed—family, work, and play. I even tried to pray at a pace no one should pray at. I think I did this because I felt that by getting a running start, I could better fling my prayers over the walls of heaven. Like that was necessary.

Thank goodness those around me have been patient. It is from them that I am learning — my brother and sister-in-law, my pastor, Dr. Westmoreland, my husband, my children. I am watching them and learning. I take walks through our garden. I'm learning the names of plants. We'll walk around the block and see how others are decorating their doors. I'll put a roast in the oven and say something like, "Supper will be ready in three hours."

It took me nearly three months to get on the right track, to find the right combination of medicine and flush away the ones that were wrong. It's taken nearly a year to learn some of the basics of slowing down. God has provided, and he has brought me through a deep and dark "blue" valley. He did it tenderly and slowly. He brought people into my life who know their chemistry, and others who know their counsel.

Yes, I could write a book about this experience, and maybe one day I will. But for now, I'm in no hurry. Wow, I never thought I'd be saying those words. A comedian knows that timing is everything. For me, now is the time to be still and know that God is God. I have taken refuge in that promise. I even wrote on one of my medicine bottles, "God is working on me in ways that I can't even see or understand. Take your medicine!"

I'm taking the time to stop and smell the roses. I'm also slowing down to listen to the laughter. There is great comfort in knowing I don't have to rush to the next punch line. There is also great comfort in knowing that should anything happen to my gallbladder, Dr. Westmoreland is close by, and his knives have already been sharpened.

ROADKILL REPORT

Fish On!

Children are a heritage from the LORD.
—PSALM 127:3

You know the theme song from that famous Clint Eastwood western *The Good, the Bad, and the Ugly*? It's whistled in the movie — a sharp little trill followed by three ominous notes. If you're a good whistler, you can do that just about anywhere and people — strangers even — will square off like they've got a pair of .45s strapped to their hips. That's what I felt like one Sunday morning in Toledo, Ohio — another Mother's Day on the road for me. I thought I could even hear the jangle of spurs as I walked into the pastor's study at 7:45 that morning, but it was only the whistling of my sinuses. We didn't get to Ohio until 2:30 that morning — about five hours before. So nothing about me was ready for a showdown.

Don't get me wrong. No one was mean to me, and I guess the gunfighter analogy begins to break down here, but so many times when I speak on Sunday mornings, I can sense a real territorial battle for the pulpit — particularly this morning, since a Mother's Day service is considered one of the "big crowd" days for a church. Preachers hate to give up their pulpits on "big crowd" days. I know this because my father and my brother were both preachers for years and I've heard the insider talk. So why would this pastor give up his pulpit to me on a "big crowd" day? Well, after all, I am a mother, with two beautiful children who can do some crazy things — some things that'll make me pull my hair out! So I could relate to just about every mother there in the big crowd.

Over all, the morning went great. Maybe I should sleep less all the time. Or maybe things went so well because I focused mainly on the two little loves of my life: my children. At that time, my daughter, Chera, was preparing for college, and my son, Zachary, was getting ready for high school. I understood that back home they had a specially crafted, handmade card and a special gift just for me. I also knew that as soon as this morning was over, I was heading to the airport to go home.

By the end of the service, I noticed the pastor was beaming. I recognized that look. I'd seen it on my husband's face before — not in church, but at his favorite fishing hole. Once, he let me try his favorite rod and reel. He passed it to me carefully on the riverbank one day, but I could tell he hated to let go. And even then he stood closer than he should have. (I nearly hooked him in the ear on one cast!) He stood and watched nervously and listened for any abnormal *clicks* or *twangs* that would indicate trouble to the reel. Then a bass nearly jerked the whole outfit from my hands, but I held on. When I pulled the big fish in using his favorite, handy-dandy fishing reel, David just beamed — the same way that preacher did that Sunday morning when I turned the pulpit back over to him. It had been a real honor, and I told him that. (Speaking, not fishing; the analogy is over!) Now I was off to the airport.

Since there were no flights leaving out of Toledo on Mother's Day afternoon, my road manager and I caught a ride to the Detroit airport, which was about an hour away. We packed into the backseat of a Ford pickup, while the woman who owned the truck and her two children rode up front. One of the kids was a teenager, and he had his Walkman headset on and was listening to *my* tape. After every joke, he'd pause the tape and ask me a question, usually something like, "Did that really happen?" And since I couldn't hear what was going on in his ears, I'd usually have to ask something like, "Did what really happen?" The mother kept asking me questions too, and I really wouldn't have minded, but she liked to look right at me when she asked them, *and she was driving!* I'd had two hours of sleep in the last forty-eight hours, but I was wide-awake now.

I finally made it back to Nashville that evening, and there to meet me at the other side of the beefed-up security were my two children, with a beautiful card, all lumpy with macaroni and toilet paper rolls, and a special gift they couldn't wait to hand off to me: my very own fishing pole. David stood behind them, just beaming.

Part 5

Dear Chonda,

You were in rare form at the Women of Faith event yesterday! Gorgeous outfit, by the way. I want those pants, but I'm gonna have to stretch them out—a lot!

Cho
123
An

ENJOY THE RIDE

Frodo: "Where are you taking us?"
Aragorn: "Into the wild."
—*THE LORD OF THE RINGS*

Life is either a daring adventure
or nothing.
—**HELEN KELLER**

ce
Lane
USA

Chapter 17

The Girls Are Back in Town — Yeah!

*M*aybe you already know that not long ago I finished up a big tour with Sandi Patty (thirty-nine Dove Awards, five Grammys, probably has the keys to a few cities in her makeup bag—*that* Sandi Patty). I wanted to call it "The Two Most Incredible Voices of All Time in One Place Tour." But my manager thought that would be too misleading. "Define 'incredible,'" I challenged him in my most incredible voice. So we finally decided on "The Girls Are Back in Town."

In eighteen months, we bounced all over the country and did about eighty shows. Before the tour set out though, we put together a garage band and shot a video after changing the lyrics of "The Boys Are Back in Town." The gist of the story is that Sandi and I decide to show our smart-aleck kids that Momma knows a thing or two about rockin' a song. In the blink of an eye, and through the magic of video, we are suddenly decked out in orange hair and leather pants. Sandi's even wearing a spiked collar! (Yes, that same Sandi Patty with all the trophies.) The whole song is over in less than three minutes, but the video took us about eight hours to make. Nothing like singing with your nose pressed up against the camera lens for four of those eight hours.

The best thing is that we took that attitude on the road with us. We may have lost the orange hair and the spiked collar, but we kept the leather pants.

I made a deal with Sandi and told her she could be in charge of wardrobe for the first half of the show. And she chose fine, satiny things to wear, with chiffon and lace and ties and bows and accessories that matched. I'd never thought about my earrings matching my pantyhose before then. Real classy.

But the second half of the show was all mine. And I chose leather pants! After that, anything else that even came close to matching was fine. Leather was a first for Sandi, and I had to beg her from the stage to come out and show them off. I'd chosen black, but hers were fire-engine red. And to match, she worked up a deep shade of blush — all natural. She looked funny trying to cover her leather-clad legs with her microphone — Hide this spot! Hide that spot! — so I hurried up and made her sing right away.

In one city after another, she kept pulling on one leather leg at a time until eventually she seemed to conquer her fears and loosen up. Could be I pushed too hard, though. With about forty shows under our matching belts, her husband, Don, went shopping with her one day and helped her pick out at least four more pairs of leather pants. Go Don! When Sandy wore her leather pants, the high notes never sounded sweeter.

Across the country we zigzagged, performing before some of the largest audiences of any genre. We made such a splash that even the gang from *Billboard* wrote about us in their usual *Billboard* sort of way: "Good Girls: 'The Girls Are Back in Town Tour' . . . continues to do strong business." See?

When I read that, I looked at Sandi and said, "Good girls? That's us, right?" She hesitated, then said, "Yes. Yes I think so."

Of all the venues, I think the arenas where they had a hockey rink stowed under the flooring were our favorite because all that ice helped take the edge off the hot flashes — sometimes for all four thousand of us. Of course, breathable cotton pants might have helped too.

Needless to say, we were both pretty excited about what was happening. Everyone involved in the tour had a real sense that we were creating not only something worthwhile but something that would last. Something that would be way bigger than what Sandi and I put together. Something *Billboard* would have to come back and write more about.

One night when we were in Indianapolis — Sandi's hometown territory — her whole family came backstage before the show, and Sandi sat me down, while her family (her hubby, mom and dad, and eight kids) formed a semicircle before me and sang "I Believe," and I thought maybe I *had* died. Maybe that temperamental curling iron had finally short-circuited and took me with it, and now I was in heaven listening to the choir. The only way I could explain Sandi and her whole family being there with me was that Sandi must have tried to save me. Her entire clan must had held hands and tried to pull me from the killer curling iron, only to fail — but at least now we were all in heaven together! That's what I was thinking as this angelic choir serenaded just me.

It was hard to do serious comedy after that, so I told the crowd about almost getting electrocuted by a curling iron. Like I said, it was hard to do comedy after that.

One of our favorite things to do before a show was to run out in our "Momma clothes" (loose cotton that's good for carpooling) and take pictures of some of the women (and the few brave, brave men) lining up to come in for the concert. Later in the show we'd flash these pictures on the big screen, and everyone would have a big time. This particular night in Springfield, Missouri, something special happened. As Sandi and I walked along the line greeting people and snapping pictures, we spotted an older couple, and right away I knew I wanted them to be my grandparents. We began to talk to them and discovered that they'd been married for fifty years. So we hugged them both, like girls do. We took their picture, and we asked her how she'd managed to get hubby to come to a pretty much all-woman concert. But before she could answer, I invited them to come live with me. And as we giggled and celebrated the time we had with this couple, the husband finally leaned close to me and, in almost a whisper, said, "Your videos have gotten us through." What? He nodded and chewed his bottom lip. "My wife has cancer, and it has progressed into her bones. She loves you, Chonda." And it was plain he loved her. That explained why he'd braved the all-woman crowd and the long wait. He did it for her.

I quickly gathered my senses and told him, "You know, I've got connections around here." Then I marched the two of them to the front of the line, through the front door, and down to a pair of seats perfect for a couple who'd been married for half a century. "So what's it like being married for fifty years?" I asked. This time the wife answered, comfortable now in her front-row seat, "If the next fifty are as wonderful as the first fifty, I can't wait."

This tour has undone me. I used to be a bit of a control freak. I don't think I was ever a jerk, just protective of everything from making sure there was plenty of toilet paper on the bus (the soft kind with the teddy bear on the package, not the pine trees) to having the right-size bulb in the spotlight. I've been a bit overwhelmed by the press, the agents, and the "record company people" who have shown up here and there to witness the combination of salon and saloon. Someone even said to me once, "Sandi has certainly brought some class to your show!" I think I even used that line later in the show—just to show everyone (and myself) that I'm all right. Then I pouted around in my spirit and let those words ring in my ears for too long.

But, you know, things change. Other than the fact that my name still gets misspelled (Chondra, Shonda, LaChonda, you name it), things of this earth change and fade away. My time with Sandi has been the biggest, most fun ride of my whole career, and I'll *never* say we've done our last show together. But already we're both looking around the next turn to see what's up ahead. Old ticket stubs we kept as souvenirs probably will be lost one day (or sold on eBay). The set pieces will be broken down to build new set pieces. The *Billboard* magazine with my name in it will one day be transferred to micro-fiche and stored away somewhere in a climate-controlled vault. And one day, maybe a thousand years from now, even those leather pants will fade away like so much cow skin.

I doubt anyone will even remember Chonda and Sandi and "The Girls Are Back in Town Tour" fifty years from now. But I'll bet you one thing: my little adopted grandparents will still be together. That kind of love will never fade. And when I get there to heaven to see them again, I hope they'll return the favor and walk me to a good seat, one right up close to the front.

ROADKILL REPORT

Momma's Farewell Crash

Honor your father and your mother.
—EXODUS 20:12

When I first starting touring, I did a little run called "Girls' Nite Out" with my sister-in-law, Doris, and my mother. Yep, Mom. We didn't have a bus back then, just flew all over the country, which wasn't too bad because as long as we had Momma, we could board early and get good seats on the plane.

We'd done at least forty cities by this time and would finish up in Minneapolis. This would be a special time for us — saying goodbye to the tour, retiring Mom, shopping at the Mall of America (only the largest mall in the country!). This was such a special time, in fact, that we went to Minneapolis a day early. Once the cab dropped us off at the mall, Doris ran ahead to find a wheelchair. That was the deal we had whenever we went anywhere with Momma and we were in a hurry: she would ride in the wheelchair and we would push. Mom could walk just fine but not very fast, and certainly not for very long. She'd finished up with her cancer treatments only shortly before this. There was no way Mom would be able to keep up with two young, shopping-savvy whippersnappers like Doris and me. And there was also no way she was ever going to get the hang of one of those motorized chairs, but that was all they had.

At first, Mom had trouble with the hand controls. She couldn't seem to understand that there was a lot of room between the forward and reverse positions. I told her over and over again: Push the stick a little, move a little. Push it a lot, move a lot — and fast. She couldn't understand this. Instead, she'd either shove the stick all the way forward or all the way back, so that everywhere she went, she zoomed. What she had was no wheelchair; it was a geriatric Harley. Talk about power shopping! She wove her chair in and out of people while at the same time snatching dresses and sweaters from racks, and at one point, she nearly ran over one of those questionnaire people who always interrupt your shopping to ask you personal questions about the shampoo you use. Mom braked long enough to explain a dandruff problem she had twenty years ago and then raced off to the next dress shop. Mom loves a new dress.

For all the troubles with the electric wheelchair, we were still glad we had it. We used her as a truck by piling things on her lap or looping bags over the chair's handles. This was a big help for Doris and me. Sometimes, when Mom was out in the open, out of the crowded shops, she looked like a runaway clothing truck (if there is such a thing). All day long these seasoned, shopping-savvy whippersnappers had a hard time keeping up with her as she left her mark there on the Mall of America — scuff marks, crash marks, skid marks. Look for them if you ever get the chance to go there.

The next morning we went to the Billy Graham Evangelistic Association headquarters, where I spoke at the chapel service. Everyone was very attentive, except for Momma. She was off looking for Billy Graham. (I was so glad we'd left the wheelchair at the mall.) Even though we'd heard he was nowhere around that day, she would not be dissuaded. Finally, she saw someone from far off who was getting into a cab and who looked like him from the back — same gray, flowing hair — and that was good enough for her, although the man could have simply been a drywall repairman heading for the Mall of America.

That night we performed our last "Girls' Nite Out" concert together. Doris played the piano as sweetly as I've ever heard her play. Mom delivered her five lines of the skit we always did (which somehow had turned into thirty-five lines by this last night), and I told the 4,500 people there that we need to get together real soon and do this again, but maybe we'd better make it a different mall, at least until the dust settles and the paint dries in Minneapolis.

Chapter 18

Milk Cows and Famous People

One weekend not too long ago, I got a good look at the face of ministry: one day it looked very much like a couple of famous people from TV, the next like a milk cow. Well, that's not completely true. First it looked like a milk cow. Then we flew to California and saw the famous people from TV.

David and I had a long four days together, which was only right since it was our nineteenth wedding anniversary. We began in the middle of nowhere, and for a long time I thought we'd never get there. First we flew into Kansas City. Fellow Christian artist Al Denson had asked me to come to this place he knows about, a place he likes to help out by doing concerts for one of "the most remarkable men he knows," named Bill. "Just fly into Kansas City, then head over to hangar twelve, and there'll be a plane waiting to take you the rest of the way," he said. So David and I did just that, but when we got to hangar twelve, there was nothing but a small jet there—large enough for about eight people. Al wasn't there, but Al's guitar player was.

"So exactly where are we going?" I asked.

The guitar player shook his head and smiled. "Oh man, it's in the middle of nowhere. But at least we have a nice ride, huh?"

It was a nice ride. The jet was sleek and had that new-jet smell. The seats were soft and leather and swiveled so we could all face each other and talk about going to the middle of nowhere. "Bill's an incredible man," the guitar player said. "He made millions in the insurance business and decided to spend most of it building this place. He wants to help troubled teenagers."

"Bill owns the middle of nowhere?" I asked.

"Yeah. He owns this jet too. He owns all sorts of things. But you'd never know it just by listening to him."

My husband asked, just as the engine began to rev up and the nose of the plane turned to face the empty expanse of runway, "Didn't Al Denson have a bad plane crash a few years ago?"

The guitar player grinned. "Man, you should have him tell you about that sometime." He shook his head. "Heck of a story."

"So where is Al?"

"He's flying the plane."

I saw David's fingers dig into the plush leather. Mine may have too.

"Just kidding," said the guitar player.

We flew for less than an hour and then landed on an airstrip in the middle of a cornfield (*If you build it, they will come . . .*). We didn't see Bill any that evening or the rest of that night. Instead, a really nice young man named John met us and showed us around. What we did see was what Bill had built. There in the middle of Missouri, a few miles outside of Kansas City, lies Heartland Ministries—a small city. There's a diner, a grocery store, a church, a giant man-made lake, a gym, and dozens of small homes that our guide told us all housed counselors and students. He also told us that Heartland Ministries was growing every day with more and more "troubled" teenagers.

"So who comes here?" I asked.

Our guide, John, smiled and said, "Have you heard the expression 'You got one last chance'? Well, these people are on that last chance. It was either here or jail for most of them. Most of these kids have done drugs, stolen to get drugs, about destroyed their families because of drugs, been in and out of jail so many times that they'd run out of chances. Their families gave up on them long ago. The judge knows Bill pretty well, and so he'll make the kids an offer in the courtroom: here for a year or jail for maybe longer. Most people choose here."

"So how did you wind up working for Bill?"

John smiled and said, "Judge Hanson asked me."

"But I thought you said you'd been here for three years."

He shrugged. "I like it here. I like the way I am now. Would you like to see the barn?"

What he was talking about was no ordinary barn, nor was it little. Turns out that this little place in the middle of nowhere is home to one of the largest dairy producers in the country. "We have over four thousand head of cattle that need to be milked twice a day," he told us. "This is as close to automatic as you can get."

Seems Bill knew some people in the engineering field as well, ones who'd designed a cow carousel for farms in Europe. That's right. The cow hops on at one spot and takes a ride in one big circle. Along the way, one person swabs her udder with what looks like a big Q-Tip and another fits her with an automatic milker. By the time she makes the loop, eight to ten minutes, she's all milked. She's then unattached and herded off, where she heads back to the field for more sweet, green grass. The milk is quickly on its way to pasteurization and homogenization and not too long after that to the trucks that will head out and cover much of the Midwest. And who works in the milk barn? Those last-chance students, that's who.

"Everyone here works," John said. "It's a required part of the program."

I saw a young girl who couldn't have been much older than my daughter. She wore a rubber apron and gloves. A cow's rear end swung by, and the girl dodged it and then leaned in as close as she could and fitted a four-prong contraption over the cow's udder. Then she leaned back out, pushed her blonde hair off her forehead with the back of her hand and dodged the next cow and repeated the process. Every so often one of the cows would deposit a fresh, steaming patty right there on the carousel. When that happened, no one would say a word, no one even screamed or said, "Oh yuck, it stinks." Before long, someone would come by and blast it away with a hose. Other than that, not a word was uttered. Everyone remained tight-lipped and kept working.

John then showed us a building that looked like an airplane hangar but inside of it were bleachers surrounding a stage. It was big and empty, and we were in the middle of nowhere. If worse came to worst, there were over four thousand cows close by, and I had lots of cow jokes.

But just like in that movie *Field of Dreams*, as night fell, the cars began to drive in on the only, long road to the place. Headlights dotted the road for what looked like miles. By the time the concert started, the once empty building was packed with teenagers. Where had they all come from? Our guitar-player friend led praise and worship, and I was afraid the place would come undone. I told some stories and the teenagers cackled, and a guest speaker shared the Word. I could imagine someone asking, "Is this heaven?"

The next morning we went back to our private jet, waiting for us in the cornfield. That's where we first met Bill. He'd missed the worship service because he'd gotten in so late the night before and was a little late this morning because he'd been praying with some of the teenagers. He was an older man of average height, with white hair and dressed in a dark suit. He would be flying back with us because he had some meetings in Kansas City. On the way back to the city, in the air, Bill told us all about Heartland — what we didn't already know.

"Did you see the lake? The grocery? The restaurant? Did you see the cows? The carousel? You know there's only three in the world like it?"

Bill was so sweet and kind and genuine that I was about ready to ask him to be my grandpa.

"Do you know how many teenagers we have now?" Before I could make a guess, I saw his eyes well up with tears. "These kids are amazing. People give up on 'em too soon. You know what the key is? Work. Oh, most of 'em still don't know it yet, but there's nothing better than honest, hard work." His hands, aged and I would guess callused as testimony to his many years of hard work, were clasped together, almost in prayer. "They stay busy here," he said. "They don't have time to think about drugs or alcohol or stealing or hurtin' anybody. I try to give 'em somethin' to do. Somethin' they can take pride in. Did you see the cows? Most kids don't know a thing about cows before they come here. I didn't even know that much. But I wanted to find something to keep them all busy. The first place they go is to the cow wheel. That's where they start. No one's too good to work the cows. Really don't have to know all that much about them. One of the most important things — something everyone learns and usually the first day out — is that if she happens to do her business at your station, the best thing you can do is to keep your mouth closed — if you know what I mean." Well, that certainly explained the tight-lipped workers in the barn.

We nodded. There's a metaphor there that I think we can all learn from, but I also think it's enough just to recognize that there is one — if you know what I mean.

Bill's story is one you won't hear much about or read about, unless you happen to be out in the middle of nowhere in Kansas or standing before Judge Hanson, all out of chances. But Bill told us something else on the plane that day that I try to remind myself of every day.

"God's will flows along like a mighty river," he said. "You can either fight against that current and wear yourself out," he made two fists with his old hands and shook them like he might do in a struggle. "Or you can jump right in and get carried away." Now he opened his fists and relaxed them and they seemed to float on an invisible current, like two large feathers. "Me? I'm going for the ride."

We said goodbye to Bill in Kansas City and caught a flight out to San Jose. It's actually pretty easy to find San Jose, but I guess a song called "Do You Know the Way to the Middle of Nowhere in Missouri?" wouldn't be as catchy.

I had to be in San Jose (still on my anniversary weekend, let me remind you!) for the taping of a TV show that aired on the West Coast called *Aspiring Women*. It went great, and my husband surprised me with a dozen roses, even walked onto the stage and presented them to me while the camera was rolling. But he did look like a kid at the cow carousel—tight-lipped, not saying a word. There were a couple of other guests on that night too, and it was good to meet them and talk about ministry.

It was late when we were finished, and I was tickled to learn that a limo would be taking David and me back to the hotel. This was still officially our anniversary weekend, and finally work could be over and our celebration could start and we could be alone. When we ducked our heads and entered the back of the long, sleek limousine, we found it was already occupied. Looks like we would be sharing a ride back to the hotel with the other show guests: John Tesh and Connie Selleca. Connie I could see as a guest on a program called *Aspiring Women*. First of all, she's a woman. She's beautiful and she's been acting for years and has done hundreds of TV shows and movies. But John Tesh? Just because he's her husband? (I'm just giving John a hard time because I saw him later at an airport and he made fun of my favorite handbag.) But I think David got him good that night, even if he didn't mean to. At the time David and I had both turned forty. He began to chat with John about John's earlier days as a news reporter in Nashville, where my husband grew up. "I used to watch you on the news when I was a kid," David said. Nothing like the "when I was a kid" line to bring someone down a few notches.

It was great talking to them both, hearing how they wanted only to minister. John is a supertalented musician and songwriter, and he was promoting his new praise and worship project. Connie told us about the limited opportunities available for a Christian actor in Hollywood. "There's a lot of things I won't do or say in a film," she said. "I came to terms with that a long time ago, and I have no problem sticking with it. I mean, I want to be in God's will. I have to move like he wants me to move."

"Sort of like a cow on a carousel?" David asked.

"Huh?" John and Connie said at the same time.

The limo ride wasn't long enough to explain.

For me, the metaphor continues to grow and to focus. Whether you're a troubled teenager, a wealthy businessman, John Tesh, or famous people on TV, the best place to be—the only place to be—to find peace and rest and a life worthwhile is in the middle of the stream that is the will of God, flowing along and not fighting against the current.

When we finally made it to the hotel late that night, there were more roses waiting for me. Happy anniversary to me!

ROADKILL REPORT

The Night of the Missing Face

The Father himself loves you.
—JOHN 16:27

I was sitting in Lynchburg, Virginia, the night before Halloween, waiting for my face. I knew I should have carried it with me, but sometimes it can be too heavy to lug around through airports all day. So I'd checked it with my luggage, and now everything was gone! And there I was, sitting in a hotel room in my dirty clothes, only a few hours from heading over to Jerry Falwell's church, and without a face. Happy Halloween to me!

I started calling my little bag with all my makeup and cleansers and tweezers and such my "face" because that's what my sister-in-law, Doris, calls it. I should have been more like her: she carries hers with her at all times, no matter what. Lose the underwear, that's okay. But don't dare lose my face!

It'd been a few hours since I'd last seen my luggage, and I was starting to smell. Ever notice how some smells can take you right back to when you were six years old?—Dad's Old Spice, Mom's White Shoulders. Remember when you used to make mud pies and you didn't care how dirty you got? Remember when you would go for days without a bath and, as far as you knew, still smell fresh? Even though your hair might be matted to the sides of your head and your teeth were growing little sweaters? Ever have so much dirt on the bottoms of your feet that you really didn't need shoes? Okay, so maybe I'm the only one who remembers all this. At any rate, the dirtier I got, the more nostalgic I was becoming.

Only twenty-four hours earlier, I had been onstage at the preconference of the Women of Faith in Charlotte, North Carolina. I had been neatly pressed, smelling good, and breathing freely with minty breath. Now I was sitting in a hotel room, playing solitaire, waiting for my luggage and face, and listening to Babbie Mason's new CD, which she gave me at the conference. It's titled *Right Where You Are*. I was so glad for that, because if God had to wait for my face too, I was in trouble.

Finally, my luggage showed up about an hour before I was supposed to be at the church. Everything was there, only it all smelled of fingernail polish. I hate it when that happens. No time to get a new blouse now. At least my leather pants were okay. I don't think you could hurt those with a wheat thrasher. And to be honest, the only reason I ever wear leather pants in the first place is not to make any sort of a fashion statement, unless "I hate to iron" is a fashion statement.

All that worrying, and I made it to the church as clean as a whistle. There was a big crowd there, and we laughed and cried. Later in the evening, I called Bev Lowry, Mark's mother, up to the stage and stood close by and listened to her sing. If I had closed my eyes, I would have sworn it was my mother up there. (And that's why I kept them open!)

Before the end of the night, and maybe because of all the looking back and remembering all the yesterdays, I had an idea I thought I would try: softly I began to sing "Jesus Loves Me." I had no music, but in my head I could hear Aunt Ruth playing along with a heavy left hand. Soon everyone joined in, as I had hoped they would. For a moment, I was six years old again. Not making mud pies this time, but singing one of my all-time favorite songs. Over the years, I must have sung it with fuzzy teeth and without any teeth, some days showered and some days stinky, with tangled hair and with mud-pie mud still under my nails. I never doubted that song then. I used to sing it at the top of my lungs. So why should I doubt it now? When I feel like I have the face that only God could love—the one on the front side of my head and not in the lost luggage room at Delta—I just sing "Jesus Loves Me," or I listen to my free Babbie Mason CD.

And as far as I could tell, no one had a clue about my near disaster. Even if I had told them, I doubt they would have cared. I even got lots of compliments on my "new" shirt—the one that matched my fingernails perfectly.

Chapter 19

Watch for
Roaming Elves

I had a few weeks off during the summer, so what did we do? We
rented an RV to go driving all over the country. Well, not the
whole country; we decided to head west. Once we made up our minds
to do just that, we laid out a big map and plotted a giant figure eight
in the reddish-orange section. It's reddish-orange on the map because
there aren't many trees west of the Rockies but lots of big, craggy
mountains. We flew into Salt Lake City, where we picked up our RV.
Before we left, David and Zachary took a quick course in plumbing:
one pipe in, one pipe out (that's about all you really need to know).
First we drove south to Zion Canyon, then on to the Grand Canyon,
then we looped up to Bryce Canyon, and finally on to Yellowstone
National Park.

When you try to write about Yellowstone, you just need too
many adjectives (colors, shapes, sizes, temperatures, animal-fur tex-
ture, etc.) Since I don't know that many, and I hate to keep repeat-
ing myself, I'll try to show you what the week was like—and most
important, I'll watch my spelling. You see, when I first wrote about
the park in my original Roadkill Report, I wanted to tell everyone
about the wildlife you can see around every turn. I wrote, "Hundreds

of buffalo and elf roam free." That's right, I said "elf." Hundreds of you wrote back, but not a single one of you to say, "Oh dear, looks like you made a typographical error." Oh no, you couldn't do that, huh? Instead, I got hundreds of letters that went something like this: "My lifelong dream has always been to see hundreds of elf roaming the prairie." Or, "Looks like that elf conservation program is working great." Or, my personal favorite, "Don't forget to brake for elves." I just want to take this moment to personally thank you so much for those kind notes. Now back to the park.

First of all, since we wouldn't know Old Faithful if it spouted up our noses, we hired a guide right away, the best guide in the whole world (or at least in Yellowstone National Park). His name is Jim Berry, and when he wants to (or when Zachary asks him politely), he can sound just like Yogi Bear. He has a really funny story about how one day he did that voice on a park ranger's radio and nearly lost his job. If you ever run into him up there, ask him about that.

Jim took us to every nook and cranny in Yellowstone, which was quite an accomplishment since Yellowstone is made entirely of nooks and crannies—over two million acres of them. He said most people who visit the park will spend an average of only thirty-six hours there; we had a whole week (which translates to about twenty rolls of film). He took us to the thermal areas first, where bottomless, clear pools of water simmer at about 180 degrees. And next to them, pools of mud will bubble up like pudding on a griddle. Zach and David kept daring each other to touch it, and Chera and I kept pulling them back. Jim told us a story about how the early settlers used to catch a trout in the lake, swing it over into one of these bubbling, clear pools for a few minutes, and then eat their supper while it was still on the hook. Jim had lots of stories like this.

He steered us right to Old Faithful. (In case you go there yourself and don't have a guide, it's the hole in the ground with all the bleachers built around it.) We got there early and got a good seat. Now, before Old Faithful does its thing, it will bubble up and shoot some short sprays into the air and everyone will lean forward on his or her seat. But when that's all that happens, everyone settles back, and you can hear this collective sigh of disappointment. When Old Faithful is not spouting 130 feet of hot water into the air, there really isn't that much to see. Quite boring, really. David's got forty-five minutes of this on video, which is even more boring to watch the second, and especially the third, time. The only thing that makes it bearable is listening to him say things like, "I think this is it! No ... no ... not yet. Do you hear something? My arm's tired. You'd think there'd be a bell or something." Yeah, we got forty-five minutes of this. At one point, David shot a close-up of the Old Faithful brochure and jiggled the camera a bit. "Just in case the battery runs out before the real thing happens," he said. Actually, that part looks really good. When we watched the replay one night after we got back, it fooled my mom—and David.

One day we went horseback riding, but not before I bought a can of pepper spray designed to ward off bears. Now, a regular can of pepper spray, the kind designed to fight off serial killers, is about the size of a pack of Certs. But pepper spray for bears comes in a can the size of a small fire extinguisher, complete with its own quick-draw holster. David made fun of me and said I was being silly. I holstered up anyway.

The horses arrived, and everyone picked their favorite one, according to color mostly. I picked Old Chief because he was old ... and he was a chief. Joan, our horseback-riding guide, said the main thing was not to pick one that had an ill-fitting saddle. I had ridden before, but it'd been years. Chera had taken lessons not long before. Zach had seen enough on TV that he hopped right up and took control of the reins with no problem. I think David had ridden less than anyone. And after about a mile on the ten-mile ride into backcountry, I was pretty sure of this.

Before we headed out, I noticed Joan had also holstered up a big can of pepper spray. "So you guys like this stuff?" I asked, slapping my own personal can as if it were a six-shooter.

Joan smiled. Then she leaned over her saddle horn, looked around as if making sure no one was listening in, and said in a low voice, "If it wasn't against the law—because we're in a national park—I'd be packing a gun." Then she straightened and nodded to punctuate how serious this venture was.

I looked at David and nodded to double punctuate how serious this venture was.

"You stay close to me," David said, and it sounded like he was concerned about my safety. But really, I think he was after my pepper spray.

Our horses were workhorses. They climbed up ridges that overlooked valleys and tittered down trails that spilled into valleys. I prayed for our horses' legs and their shoes and that the rocks they stepped on were nice and firm. Every now and then Joan would point out long, jagged rips in the tree bark, about chest high when you're sitting on a horse.

"Grizzlies," she said, and in a grizzled manner.

I noticed that every time we saw these markings, she'd take her reins into her left hand, then slide her right hand a little closer to her pepper spray. So did I. David horsed over closer to me. Once, when all the horses came to an abrupt stop on their own, Joan raised her hand and hushed us all. I think we even stopped breathing.

"I hope it's a bear," Zach whispered.

"That's not funny," Chera said. "Dad can't ride that well."

Up ahead a giant black moose stepped out onto the trail, and following closely behind was a giant gray baby moose. We watched them and they watched us for several long minutes. A moose is so gangly and ungraceful even standing still, with its big body and skinny legs and knobby knees. David shifted around in his saddle and could not get comfortable enough to be still for more than half a minute. I don't think it fit him so well. When the moose finally moved on, the kids wanted to gallop, so Joan kicked her horse and the kids followed.

Now, the thing about trail horses is that they each do what the one in front does. So when Zach and Chera galloped away, so did Mom and Dad. I'm not sure it was so much David's saddle that was ill-fitting as it was David. As he galloped ahead of me, I saw enough daylight between him and his saddle to herd a moose through. He yelped, and this probably did more to shoo the bears away than the pepper spray ever could. The kids pulled up, and David's horse stopped, with him clinging desperately to its side. Fortunately, the trailhead was close, and we made it back to the RV without injury or being eaten. The worst that happened on our little horse trip was that David walked bowlegged for the next three days.

That week we saw elk and buffalo and foxes and coyotes and moose. We pulled over once and watched an eagle perched in its nest. We swatted big mayflies out of the air and tossed them over the edge of Fisherman's Bridge and watched giant brown trout rise to pick them off the surface. We got caught up in a few "animal jams," which were far more slow-moving than any freeway traffic I've ever been caught in back home. In Yellowstone, when someone spots an animal (deer, buffalo, even a squirrel), he pulls over and grabs a camera. So does the person behind him. And so does the person behind him. Traffic can back up for miles because a buffalo suddenly decides to scratch its back in a dirt spot by the road. But unlike in the traffic jams back home, no one loses patience or gets angry. It's an understanding out West, in the middle of nature at its wildest. People there know they're in a special place, where nature shows off in ways you won't see anywhere else in the world. And if one is patient (and has a full tank of gas), he can witness one of God's greatest shows.

We never saw a bear the whole time we were there. "Too hot," Jim told us. And this reminded him of the big fire of '88, when nearly half of the 2.5 million acres were destroyed. "It was a sad time," he said. It was easy to see the places that had been scarred. In these places, blackened timbers still lay crisscrossed, and the earth beneath was the color of charcoal. But there was no doubt about what the short pine trees that spotted the gray hillsides meant: "It's coming back," Jim said. "The forest." And he smiled broadly. "It's such a short growing season, that it'll take some time." It'd already been fifteen years, and the trees weren't much taller than me. But God was growing them, slowly and patiently. We learned that Jim was a man of faith, but admittedly his faith had dwindled over the years. Whittled away over time, the way he explained it. Then he told us a story about a pine seed, a pod of pine seeds actually. "These pods filled with seeds are pretty much sealed up with so much sap that they never open up to disperse their seeds."

"Then where did all these trees come from?" my kids wanted to know.

"Oh, the pods will open," Jim said. "It just takes a lot of heat to melt the sap—like a fire. You set fire to one of those, it'll open up and spread seeds like popcorn. Amazing how it does that. A fire destroys the whole place, but it's the fire that causes the new trees to grow." He shook his head, as if he were trying to figure out one of those tough math word problems I used to fail in middle school.

"God is so cool," Chera said.

Jim smiled and even nodded. No one would say, but I think God was growing Jim's faith back, like some of the short pine trees sprouting up around us—slowly and patiently. I thought about the fires I'd been through: my parents' divorce, the death of my sisters, financial hardships. How had the heat from those blazes opened up new seeds for me? New friendships, stronger faith, valuable experiences. You may never forget the fires, but neither can you overlook the new growth that comes afterward, or the seeds of new possibilities that spread out like popcorn!

We hated to leave Yellowstone, but we'd run out of time for this trip. We packed up the RV and waved goodbye to deer and buffalo and eagles and moose and trout and would have been out in twenty minutes if it hadn't been for getting caught in one last animal jam. David put the RV in park, and we sat and waited for our turn to move up and see what it was that God had going on this time. For the next hour, we crept along for no more than two hundred yards. But the wait was well worth it. For off to the side, in a long expanse of a green valley, grazed a herd of beautiful roaming elves.

ROADKILL REPORT

Almost Famous

To him [God] be the glory forever!
—ROMANS 11:36

It was cold and dark, and I was tired—oh wait, haven't I written this before? Oh well, the rest of this story will be quite different. We'd begun a five-day run with a new bus driver, who I'll call Chuck. I could tell Chuck was not happy. He would have rather been out with somebody like Metallica. Someone more famous. I could tell because he would moan and groan whenever we stopped for snacks (like we do whenever we can) and got back on the bus with cookies and popcorn and Diet Pepsi and malted milk balls (boy, those never lasted very long)—and no beer. Chuck wanted beer.

I could also tell he wasn't happy to be driving my bus because when there was a way to pull up close to the hotel so we wouldn't have to drag our luggage quite so far, Chuck would park way in a back corner of the parking lot and make us walk three blocks, in the loose gravel. Maybe he was afraid someone would park next to his bus and ding it with a car door.

And I could tell that Chuck wasn't too happy about shuttling us around because whenever we'd get back to the bus after a show, we had to take the Metallica CD out so we could listen to Darlene Zschech's greatest hits. No, Chuck didn't seem to care too much for our snacks, or our music, or the fact that nobody on this particular bus ride was all that famous.

Chuck also had a need for speed. And as will often happen when you fly down the interstate above the speed limit in a giant bus at three in the morning, the law will pull you over and give you a ticket. That's what happened to us somewhere in the northern part of New York. I woke when the bus stopped, and I shuffled out to see what was going on, especially since I could hear Chuck talking to somebody. Chuck didn't like to talk to most people.

When I slid the door to the front cabin open, I could see blue lights flashing through the curtains. Uh-oh. I slipped quietly back to my bunk and waited. Let Chuck handle this, I thought. That's what he's paid for. And if he's gotten caught speeding, then that's his problem. For a long time, everything was real quiet, and I was beginning to fear that maybe the law had taken our Chuck downtown for fingerprints and had abandoned us there on the side of the highway.

I rapped on the tour manager's bunk. Maybe he should get up and see what was taking so long. (Which is what *he* gets paid to do!)

Just then the door that separates the bunk area from the front sitting area slid open. "Ahh ... Chonda," someone whispered. Chuck? Chuck never talked to me.

"Yes?"

"I ... ah ... do you have any of those pictures I saw earlier ... of you?"

It *was* Chuck. I wondered what he was up to. "Yeah, I think so. Look out there on the table, by the Oreos."

I heard him poke around. I heard the plastic crinkling sound of moving snacks. Then Chuck was back at the door. "Chonda?"

"Yeah?"

"Do you think you could autograph one of these?"

"What's going on, Chuck?"

I heard a deep sigh. "It's the officer."

"You got stopped?" I suddenly felt like a terrible actor.

Another deep sigh came from Chuck. "Seems this officer's wife is a big fan of yours." Sigh. "He'd like an autographed picture."

I tried hard not to laugh. "All he wants is a picture?"

One more sigh. (What is the record for the most sighs in a one-minute span?) "Your road manager's getting some CDs and DVDs out of the bay now. We worked out a deal," he said, while blue lights flashed behind him. "So if you don't mind signing this ..."

Chuck was as sweet as a malted milk ball after that. And for the rest of that five-day run, he parked closer to the hotel doors, he didn't fiddle with my praise and worship music, and I was the most famous person he knew.

Part 6

Dear Chonda,

I just know the day is coming when I'll have to wear Depends because you make me laugh so hard. Keep it up, girl!

Chon
123
Any

ce
Lane
USA

HOMEWARD BOUND

We shall not cease from exploration
And the end of all our exploring
Will be to arrive where we started
And know the place for the first time.
—T. S. ELIOT

There's no place like home.
There's no place like home.
—DOROTHY, IN *THE WIZARD OF OZ*

Chapter 20

DucK Heaven

*I*n Memphis, Tennessee, they have these famous ducks. Maybe you've heard of them? They live at the Peabody Hotel there in downtown Memphis. But these aren't just any ducks; they're as near to royalty as you can get! Every day, since the 1930s, five nicely groomed and trained mallards (one drake and four hens) will make their way from their penthouse apartment, down a special elevator reserved just for them, and into the lobby. Then they are led by the red-and-gold-jacketed Duckmaster down a fifty-foot run of red carpet, to the music of John Philip Sousa's "King Cotton March," to the fountain in the main lobby. Here they splash around all day before being led back up to the roof in the late afternoon. That's not a bad gig, is it? To me, it looks pretty much like duck heaven. What duck wouldn't want to live in a penthouse suite, swim all day in the opulence of a five-star (five-duck, according to the website) hotel? Yeah, for ducks, heaven is the Peabody Hotel in Memphis.

I got so caught up in all the pomp and circumstance that I tried to get one of the duck's autograph. I thought the Duckmaster was going to blow an epaulet (you know, those gold things on the jacket shoulders that look sort of like gold hairbrushes?). So I did the next best thing: I brought home all the duck-shaped soaps from the bathroom. I gave them to my manager, since he's a big duck hunter. (Of course, I never let word of *that* leak out while I was there.)

The beginnings of this duck ritual should come as no surprise: alcohol was involved. Seems the general manager back in the 1930s was a big duck hunter too, and back then you could use live decoys to hunt ducks. He came in late one night, didn't feel like putting away the decoys, and so he marched them into the hotel lobby and bedded them down in the fountain. The guests loved it so much that the manager had to give up his decoys, but he did gain a nice pair of epaulets.

We were riding the bus back from Memphis when I got a call from my very best friend from high school. She called to tell me that her mother had finally lost her battle with cancer and wanted to know if I would sing at her funeral—and tell some jokes. I'm not kidding. I reminded Meribeth that the last time I worked in a funeral home, I got fired (seems the microphone in the little room we were tucked away in to sing our songs was still on when I first started writing some of my favorite funeral jokes). But Meribeth knows exactly what it is I do and the kinds of things I say, and she knows that in the end I will tell people about heaven. And if this many of her mom's best friends and family were going to be gathered, she wanted to make sure she got the message out that this place is not our home. So I said sure and made certain to strike out the funeral jokes. Anyway, Meribeth was glad that I was going to be there.

Meribeth and I go back over twenty-five years, back to when we were both small enough to fit inside a book locker, where we would sometimes hide until the halls were clear. And I'm not talking about those sports lockers built for shoulder pads and all. I'm talking about those skinny, skinny lockers that'll barely hold a science book and a history book at the same time. I used to fit in one of those. If you don't believe me, check out the Cheatham County Central High School annual, 1978, page 2. That's me tugging Meribeth out of locker number 112. We got caught that day, but most of the time we got away with it. We skipped so much chemistry together that year that I couldn't even begin to tell you what a ribonucleic acid is. Meribeth was voted Mrs. CCCHS that year. I got Most Talented (and it had nothing to do with that locker—although today it most definitely would, providing I could still do it). My husband, David, was voted Mr. CCCHS. He and Meribeth like to remind me that technically they were married first.

So that's how close Meribeth and I are. And that's why she wanted me to "do my thing" at her mother's funeral.

Once everyone had taken a seat and seemed as comfortable as possible dressed in their most "respectable" outfits, I told them the locker story and people laughed. It was a good room. I sang a song about heaven and everyone cried—at least I did. I thought about the ducks at the Peabody Hotel and almost told that story. But then I told them a story about my husband and son and how once while watching the World Series together one year, Zachary asked, "Hey, Dad, what does the winning team get?"

David grinned and said, "Well, the winning team gets a trophy, and everybody on the team gets a gold ring and a wad of cash."

"A trophy, a ring, and a wad of cash?"

David nodded. "A trophy, a ring, and a wad of cash," he repeated.

"Wow!"

That's not too shabby an incentive for winning, is it?

Not long after that, they were watching the summer Olympics, and during the playing of the national anthem, Zachary said, "How much cash did he win?"

David shook his head and said, "All he gets is a medal and they play his country's national anthem."

"That's it? A medal and a song?"

"That's pretty big. See how he cries?"

And sure enough, tears were streaming down the big man's face as he sang every word to "The Star-Spangled Banner." And of course, as most grown-ups know, it wasn't really even the song that did it. It was what the song must have meant to him—all the work, the obstacles overcome along the way, the moments of self-doubt, the hurts, the disappointments, and finally the victory. Meaning like that would fill books and books. No wad of cash could touch that.

I told my captive funeral audience that story, and they just stared blankly back at me—I'm sure waiting for it all to make some sense for such a time as this. So I took a stab at it.

"Seems we all need something to push us toward the goal. For some, it's a ring, a trophy, and a wad of cash. For others, a medal and a song. We who strive toward heaven have Jesus. And we have brothers and sisters and friends and daddies and now, Meribeth, you have your mom. We want to wind up at the final ceremony with our friends and our family. To be reunited with those we love will be our medal. And the song? I can only imagine, but I'm sure it will be more than an instrumental, and it'll probably make me cry."

As I watched Meribeth tear up, I tried to put myself in her place. My mother is very much alive, but one day we'll meet on the other side. I stood there and tried to imagine what that will be like: There will be a long red carpet, and music will play, and Momma will make her way to me—faster, now that her knee will be all better. The music will swell. Someone will be wearing epaulets. And as she gets closer, I wouldn't doubt that Mom might even waddle just a bit.

And even though I thought it, I'm so glad that I didn't do the duck story at my little funeral talk. I would save "Duck Heaven" for later. Friend or no friend, Meribeth probably would have fired me.

ROADKILL REPORT

Bonjour! Bonjour!

And the peace of God,
which transcends all understanding,
will guard your hearts and your minds
in Christ Jesus.
—PHILIPPIANS 4:7

All I really wanted to do was get a blouse ironed. My family and
I were in Dakar, Senegal, a city of about three million people
that's located in the westernmost point of Africa. I was there at
the request of World Vision, a relief organization that has helped
millions over the last fifty years by drilling wells and providing
schooling, as well as food, medical relief, and supplies where needed.
Wherever I go, I try to tell people about World Vision, so part of
the purpose of this trip was to shoot some video and bring it back
to America. We'd traveled over six thousand miles and twenty-four
hours, and everything I had was as wrinkled as wrapping paper the
day after Christmas. Now, I know it might seem like such a petty
thing to fret about a wrinkled shirt when people in that country
need food so they might live another day, but the best way I could
help for now was with my words, on video. So I needed a nicely
pressed shirt.

Someone from the hotel where we were staying had said laundry
services were available, and so I thought I would give that a try.
Press one shirt? No problem, they said. So I sent it down plenty

early enough. But with only a half hour to go before the shoot, my shirt had not come back. I called the front desk, admittedly a bit panicked. Now, the people of Senegal speak mainly French. I speak Southern. We were having a hard time communicating. But I must have done okay because with ten minutes to go, there came a knock at my door. I pulled the door back to reveal a nice young man standing there with my freshly pressed blouse and a brilliant smile. I smiled right back, clapped and squealed, and took my shirt and said, "Bonjour!" It was late in the afternoon.

He nodded and grinned.

"Oh, bonjour!" I said again, waggling the freshly pressed shirt to show him what I was so grateful about. My husband tipped him nicely. Actually, I took the money and placed it in the young man's hand and gave it a big, thankful shake. "Bonjour! Bonjour! Bonjour!" I said for the last time, just to show him how really grateful I was. He seemed to grin the biggest yet as he backed out the door.

After he'd gone, my daughter, Chera, who'd taken at least a couple of years of high school French stepped out of the bathroom and asked, "Did you just say 'Good morning' to that man like a thousand times?"

I went wide-eyed. My French was horrible. Worse; it was nonexistent. I thought I knew at least how to say thank you. Obviously I didn't. "I don't know," I said. "Did I?"

Chera grinned and nodded. "Oui, oui."

"That means yes?"

Oh, I was embarrassed. Even though I knew I might never see that man again, I was still embarrassed. But he had grinned back at me like he'd understood. He'd nodded like he'd understood. I like to think that more than my words, he understood my actions — me waggling the shirt and smiling, me squealing and clapping my hands, me shaking his hand, me grinning and nodding and calling out "Good morning!" over and over again. Put all these actions together, and I think you have one big "Thank you."

For someone who makes her living using tens of thousands of words a day, I'll be the first to admit that, more than with words, we communicate with our actions. If we say one thing and do another, our actions will be what people hear the most. But don't expect me to spread that around too much. I make a living using words — thousands of them a day. The last thing I want is one day to be replaced by a mime.

Chapter 21

Anyone Happen to See the Grand Canyon around Here?

I wonder what the first explorers who came across the Grand Canyon must have said—besides, "Oops. Watch your step!"

And they must have tried all sorts of names before deciding on the one: Red Canyon? No. Purple? No. Rugged? How about Deep? Wide? Expansive Canyon? Bigger Than a Barn Canyon? And although they finally decided on Grand, even that is an understatement. But somehow it works. Maybe because the name's so general it allows you to mentally dredge up every adjective you could possibly think of, and with a canyon this big, the more the better. Just for fun, I pretended that I was one of the first explorers and tried to come up with my own name: God's Footprint, Heaven's Nature Bowl, Rocks and Things. Why do all my names sound like shops in a mall?

My family and I were headed to the North Rim of the Grand Canyon—the side they say is less crowded, less commercial. We were somewhat surprised to find the giant canyon in the middle of the woods. One moment we were driving along a winding, twisting road through the trees, and the next we were at the Grand Canyon Park entrance. I guess I was expecting miles of desert, like on TV.

"So where is it?" Zach wanted to know. "If it's supposed to be so big, how come we can't see it from here?"

"You know how these parks are," David said, as if he knew how these parks are. "The entrances are usually miles away from what it is you're looking for. Lots of room out West, you know." (This was his Tennessee perspective talking now, highly influenced by his cable TV experiences.) "Covered wagons aren't like compact cars," he went on as we drove. "They need a lot of room to —" We'd only driven a couple of hundred more yards, and there was the parking lot.

"So where is it?" Zach said again.

"Well, let's just take a walk and see," David said. "They're not going to let anyone park right next to the canyon. Too dangerous. You know how these national parks are."

Simple signs in the parking lot directed us to the Rim. That sounded to us like the edge of something, so we followed that. A winding trail led us through a quiet woods. There were other people there, but all were hushed, like sermon time at church, or worse, a library!

A little farther down, we saw a hippie fellow — long hair, a T-shirt with the American flag on the back, sandals. He stood on a rock wall with his back to us and held his arms outstretched like an eagle, his ponytail swinging between his shoulder blades, blowing along with the image of the flag on the back of his shirt. He looked like he might jump or like he was hoping to catch something.

Chera whispered, "I think he's looking at the canyon." We still couldn't see it from where we were.

"Is he trying to fly?" Zach whispered back.

David readied his camera.

I believe this whole trip — these years on earth — is like one long walk through the woods, until one day we step into a clearing that is heaven. Approaching the Grand Canyon the way we did that day was good practice for us for that. In a moment, in the twinkling of an eye, the trees, the ground, the whole world before us seemed to suddenly disappear into a mile-deep canyon rifled with textures and colors that stole our breath and our words away all at once. I'd seen Zach giddy with excitement before, like when we first saw the castle in Disney World. I'd seen Chera squeal and clap her hands when Mickey Mouse draped an arm about her shoulders for a photograph. But I don't think I've ever seen either of them so moved that they were rendered motionless. David finally got the video camera going, and he slowly panned it from left to right and back again, and whatever it was he found to say, he whispered every word.

Seeing it for the first time, I realized that *grand* falls so short. But I imagine the word *heaven* will as well.

Camping at the Grand Canyon is so popular that you have to make reservations a year in advance. Who makes reservations at a campground a year in advance? Obviously, everyone there that day except us. The place was full, and the nearest campground was like an hour away. "Of course," the park ranger said, his elbows resting on the window sill of our RV, his Smokey Bear hat filling the frame of the window, "seeing as how you've got your own toilet with you, you could camp at one of the remote overlooks."

"What's that? Where's that?" David asked.

"Drive back outside the park entrance. Take the first right. It's a graveled road, so it may be a bit rough. You know how national parks are." I saw David nod. "You can camp anywhere along the way."

"How much?" David asked.

"It's a national park," the ranger said. "It's free. Your tax dollars at work for you. Now, if you go to the end, about twelve miles, there's a beautiful spot there."

"It's free?" David asked.

"And beautiful." He tipped the brim of his hat and backed out of our window, and we were off.

We found the graveled road, just like he'd said. And we hadn't gone a mile before the RV began to shake like a can of paint in one of those paint shakers at Home Depot. David drove all of fifteen miles per hour while Chera, Zachary, and I hung on for dear life. But we figured this was a small price to pay for a chance to see such beauty, especially free beauty.

The twelve miles of washboard road threatened to shake out my fillings. Too bad our tax dollars hadn't stretched far enough for asphalt. Thankfully, the fillings stayed put, but a single bolt dropped out from somewhere — landed on the kitchen floor and rolled back and forth across the vinyl like the ebb and flow of an ocean tide. No one wanted to let go of what they were holding on to in order to stop it. Later we nabbed the thing and tried to figure out just where it'd come from, but it was a mystery we'd never solve. David determined it must have been an extra one we didn't need anyway. "You know how RVs are," he said. To hear him talk, RVs were full of extra bolts.

The road ended at a turnaround, and off to one side was a neat little fire circle made of rocks, with some unburned logs stacked next to it. Just a few paces beyond that was a canyon — *the* canyon. I couldn't believe we could drive this close to the edge of the Grand Canyon. If you buy a hot cup of coffee at McDonald's, it comes with a warning label: "Caution: Hot." But here at the edge of the Grand Canyon there was no supervision, not even a guardrail or a sign that said, "Danger: Driving into the canyon could be hazardous to your health." To be honest, I was a little nervous. Even one of those velvet ropes like they have in banks would have been nice.

We had the whole place to ourselves. So while David and the kids built a fire, I prepared the steaks. When I brought them out to the little grill, we laid them over the fire, and David and I said at the same time, "It just doesn't get any better than this." We watched the sun set and the canyon turn from a pink to a burning reddish orange to a deep purple and all those colors in between that have probably never even been named. We sat by the campfire, wrapped in complete darkness and blankets from the RV. We couldn't see the canyon anymore, but the lay of the land must have been imprinted on our minds like on photo paper, so that even when we stared off into complete darkness, we were just as captivated. We couldn't see it, but we knew it was there. And that knowledge of its presence brought us awe. "This is the best campsite ever," Zachary said.

Chera, and not the canyon, echoed back, "Yeah."

The next morning we watched the sun come up and watched its warm light nibble away at the edges of the shadow that reached to the bottom of the canyon. We traveled the washboard road back to the park and had dinner in the restaurant that overlooked the canyon. Here, at least, there were protective rails to make the clumsy (like me) breathe easier. After dinner, we walked out to an area where there must have been at least a hundred rocking chairs. They were filled with people happy to just sit and rock and stare into the changing colors of the canyon as the sun set. We took lots of pictures, and when we got them back, they all looked like postcards. We took several pictures of the kids walking out onto skinny overlooks—the kind Wile E. Coyote steps out on with his Acme binoculars to scan the horizon for the Road Runner. These photos looked as if we'd shrunk the kids and attached them to a postcard. I took at least three pictures of David, and in every one he's dangling the car keys over the canyon. His picture looks like one of those funny postcards with a caption like, "Wish you were here. Oops! Because it looks like we'll be here awhile!"

While sitting in one of the many rocking chairs that faced the magnificent canyon, I thought that maybe a good name for the canyon would be Almost Heaven Canyon. And I wasn't just thinking about the canyon itself, either, but also about the journey we'd made to get there. As a family, traveling companions, we'd traveled over hills and valleys together, through deserts and forests. Over smooth highways where we'd laughed and played the ABC game and over corrugated roads that had shaken us to the core. Sometimes we were surprised by what had turned up around the last bend in the road. We'd missed important turns and had to turn around before we could get stuck in places we never should have been. Sometimes we rolled the windows down and turned the music up loud and had a blast. Other times we'd grown hungry and tired, even restless. Even the grown-ups had asked, "Are we there yet?" But once we'd gotten there, once we'd witnessed its grandness and vastness, and the wind that blew up from its bottomless depths blew across our faces, it seemed as if we'd always been there. As if that was the only life we'd ever known. And I think that's how heaven will be. There'll be no roadkill in heaven.

Almost Heaven Canyon would be a good name, I thought. Plus, I couldn't think of any mall stores with that name.

When we finally left, we walked the winding path back to the RV. That hippie dude was still there—same hair, same sandals, same flag picture on his T-shirt. He even stood on the same stone wall as before, with his arms outstretched like wings, ready to fly. He was both captivating and mysterious, and he made us whisper when we walked by.

He made me nervous by standing on the wall like that. I wanted to tug on his shirt and tell him about all the wonderful rocking chairs back at the restaurant. I also wanted to know his name — for future references, such as this. Without his name, my story has one big hole. But I was afraid that if I said anything or tapped him on the shoulder, I might spook him and ... well, he was standing at the very edge of the Grand Canyon. So we let him be.

But later, when we talked about our experiences, Zachary called him "the Grand Canyon Dude." Yeah, that was a lot better than what I'd come up with: American Eagle.

Epilogue
Unpacking

Though we travel the world over to find the beautiful,
we must carry it with us or we find it not.
—RALPH WALDO EMERSON.

I never travel without my diary.
One should always have something sensational
to read in the train.
—OSCAR WILDE

*A*nd so we come to the end of this journey. How many roadkill did you count (not counting me in chapter 16)? Chances are you learned something about me—that I'm not a morning person, that I like funnel cakes, and that I don't always feel funny. But as with all good journeys, I hope you learned something about yourself as well, about what sort of a traveler you might be.

For me, when I'm on those long stretches of highway, where the road is smooth and straight and the car practically drives itself, I think about things like—laundry, Zachary's orthodontist appointment, that gray hair I thought I saw that morning, but then again the lighting was bad and maybe it was only a shadow. It's on those winding, bumpy roads, over potholes and washed-out places, rolling along in dangerously loose gravel or climbing steep hills, that I learn

the most. That's when I wonder, do I have enough gas? Where's
the next rest stop? Did I pay that last life-insurance policy? When's
the last time I told my husband I love him? When's the last time
I showed God I love him? Where's that map?—Get my point?
Some of life's most important lessons are experienced on the worst
of roadways.

We're all on a journey. Sometimes we get to share a ride for a
bit—like you taking the time to read this book. Much of the time,
though, you may feel like you're in a rental RV, barreling down the
highway with a bunch of loony people you call family. Sometimes
you may feel you're traveling on foot and all alone, weary from walking uphill, in the snow, barefoot. However you travel, you can't deny
that we're on a journey. It may be tough and long, and you may even
feel lost some days. But no matter what, you can always find a way
to enjoy the trip.

My husband will always sit by the window on an airplane. No
matter how many times he flies, he'll cozy up with his nose pressed
to the glass and watch the clouds zip by, squint at the people who look
like ants, and if we ever fly over any mountains—watch out, he'll get
loud and squirmy. He soaks it all in. I think he's the saddest when
we take a flight and our seats are over the wing. Then he spends his
time with his face pressed up to the gap between the seats in front of
us, trying to see through the window of the row in front of us. He's
determined not to miss a thing.

And the best way to enjoy the journey is to share it with someone. When a bill is past due, do you hold on to your spouse and say,
"We'll catch up"? When your kids come home with a failing grade,
can you say, "All right then, let's figure this one out together"? And if
it seems you're going in circles, all alone without a map, is there someone you can say to, "Hey, a little help here"? I don't think we were
meant to travel alone. We need traveling companions—our spouses,

children, or friends. Besides, it's always good to have someone who can help with the luggage.

Speaking of luggage. When I unpack my suitcase at the end of a long trip, it can get ugly. My goal is always to empty the thing as quickly and as thoroughly as possible. And even though it might not look like it at first, I do have a system. First, I'll zip open the top and pluck out the things that will have to be washed — the "dirties." I'll fling them to a pile over by the window. Next, I'll pluck and fling the "maybe dirties" over by the dresser. Things still folded go on the bed. Shoes over there by the bathroom door. Socks next to the shoes. And across from that, my face (remember the Roadkill in chapter 18?). When I'm finished, I've built what looks like a small clothing village with crisscrossing streets that take up the whole room. David walked in the other day and said, "Whoa, are we having a yard sale?" But I just don't feel like I'm really home from a trip until my suitcase is completely empty — completely unpacked — and David can bury it back in the attic insulation.

I guess I could make a metaphor here about all the lessons I've learned on the road — metaphorically pull each one from my traveling bag and pile them up like so much dirty laundry, huh? But there's no need for that. Besides, that suitcase is still in the trunk of the car, too heavy to lug in — even for David. I think I'll leave it out there for the next trip. After all, I am still traveling, still learning, still packing away all those lessons of the road. (Well, looks like I went and made a metaphor after all.)

And you can be sure that while I'm traveling about, I'll be paying particularly close attention to the roadkill — real and metaphorical. I'll be counting them all the way to heaven.

NEW FROM CHONDA PIERCE

*Also available in VHS

"I want to live my life so that every morning
when I wake up Satan says, 'Oh no! She's awake!'"

www.chonda.org

I Can See Myself in His Eyeballs

God Is Closer Than You Think

Chonda Pierce

What would it be like to get so close to God that we could see ourselves in his eyeballs? What if we could see our image reflected there because we were so close to him? Chonda Pierce wants to get close enough to God to see herself as God sees her. But to move closer to God, we first have to see him. In this audio book, Chonda, with her usual Southern humor, tries to open her own eyes and the eyes of the listener wide enough to see God. Where is God when her husband gets a speeding ticket, when her daughter wrecks her grandfather's truck, when there's a tragic plane crash, or when she's driving down the road in a Chevette held together by wire hangers? Come along and laugh with Chonda as she tries to catch God at work in the most unlikely places.

Audio Download, Abridged 0-310-26063-9

Pick up a copy today at your favorite bookstore!

ZONDERVAN®

GRAND RAPIDS, MICHIGAN 49530 USA

WWW.ZONDERVAN.COM

It's Always Darkest Before the Fun Comes Up

Chonda Pierce

Life might be no joke right now—but laughter is on the way. There are two kinds of laughter. One is hollow hilarity that masks pain far too deep for words. The other is a full, joyous laugh that sounds triumphantly on the far side of life's dark passages. Comedian Chonda Pierce knows both kinds. In *It's Always Darkest Before the Fun Comes Up*, this spunky preacher's daughter will do more than tickle your ribs. She'll touch the place in you where laughter and tears dwell side by side. She'll show you the deep wisdom of a merry heart. And with humor and honesty, she'll reveal the God who knows how to turn life's worst punches into its most glorious punch lines—in his perfect time.

Softcover 0-310-22567-1

Pick up a copy today at your favorite bookstore!

GRAND RAPIDS, MICHIGAN 49530 USA

WWW.ZONDERVAN.COM

For other products (DVDs, videos, CDs, cassettes, etc.) by Chonda Pierce, visit www.chonda.org or call 888-294-5459.

For concert availability, call Matt Kroeker at 615-293-1533.

For management contact:

Nicole Carpenter
615-250-3633
1025 16th Ave South
Suite 303
Nashville, TN 37212

We want to hear from you. Please send your comments about this book to us in care of zreview@zondervan.com. Thank you.

GRAND RAPIDS, MICHIGAN 49530 USA

ZONDERVAN.COM/
AUTHORTRACKER